FUNDAMENTALS

OF

HAWAIIAN
MYSTICISM

CHARLOTTE BERNEY

THE CROSSING PRESS
FREEDOM, CALIFORNIA

*This book is dedicated to my teachers, Josephine and
Jack Gray, who gave me Huna—the gift of a lifetime;
to my wonderful parents, Helen and Elvin Daigle;
and to my beloved husband, Carl.*

© 2000 by Charlotte Berney
Cover and interior design by Courtnay Perry
Cover art by Dietrich Varez
Printed in the USA

For information on bulk purchases or group discounts for this and other Crossing
Press titles, please contact our Special Sales Manager at 800/777-1048.

Visit our Web site on the Internet: **www.crossingpress.com**

Library of Congress Cataloging-in-Publication Data

Berney, Charlotte.
    Fundamentals of Hawaiian mysticism / by Charlotte Berney.
        p. cm.
    Includes bibliographical references and index.
    ISBN 1-58091-026-2 (pbk.)
      1. Huna. I. Title.
BF1623.H85 B47 2000
299'.9242—dc21   99-088516

Acknowledgments

I would like to acknowledge Marcia Noren, the catalyst for this book, as well as those who gave me valuable assistance by commenting on the manuscript: Jeanie Forte, Carl Berney, E. Otha Wingo, and John Bainbridge. Thanks also to the members of Huna Research I have known and worked with over the years and with whom I have exchanged much Huna information. I count many of them as close friends. *Mahalo* to Kawehilani Lucas, my Hawaiian language teacher; to all the teachers in Hawaii, past and present, who help others through their work; and to Serge King for his dedication to making Hawaiian knowledge available. I would like to express my appreciation of Herb Kawainui Kane for his paintings, books, and expertise that have added so much to our knowledge of historical Hawaii. Finally, *mahalo nui loa* to the Hawaiian people whose spirit of aloha is the inspiration for this book.

Table of Contents

Foreword

The mysterious, the exotic, the apocalyptic, the inexplicable, the enigmatic, the ineffable, the secretive, the "occult" (hidden), the cryptic, and the mystical have fascinated mankind from time immemorial. The Eleusinian Mysteries of the Greeks and the Mithraic Mysteries of the Persians were established institutions in those societies. Intimations of dark and forbidden rites abounded to excite the emotions and imagination of the masses and to elicit vague fears about practices unknown and misunderstood. In our own era, irrational "End Times" televangelists, newsmongers, and movies fan these emotions into panic. Some people are attracted to anything that appears strange and exotic.

In the midst of such confusion and disorder in other parts of the world, there existed the quietly powerful, natural, balanced, and practical system of Hawaiian mysticism that was a way of life for the Hawaiians and other Polynesians. It required neither belief nor speculative theories. It was an experience involving emotion, rational intelligence, and the divine, as integral parts of each person. It was characterized by a balanced view of body, soul, and spirit that considered all things natural, not "sacred," which implies that some things were separated from everyday life. There was not the "mystical union" often associated with mysticism. The experience was direct communication at every level, including the divine. Higher powers were recognized, and there was ready communication with them through their own divine nature. Although Hawaii has long been considered exotic and mysterious, the manner of living was natural and unpretentious for a setting so paradisiacal. When the influx of foreign cultures brought drastic changes to the entire society, Hawaiian mysticism had to be practiced in secret.

When Max Freedom Long went to Hawaii as a teacher in 1917, the secrets were all but lost. Stories about fantastic feats of the ancient practitioners, the kahuna, so intrigued him that he spent the next fifty-two years researching their practices. This "synthesized system," gleaned from Hawaiian sources and concepts combined with his own knowledge and experiences, he named Huna, from the word in the Hawaiian language meaning "secret" or "private family wisdom." Long clearly stated that the Huna principles, which he published as a practical system for all to use, were not synonymous with the traditional religious practices of the ancient Hawaiians. The Huna system is based on principles recovered from those practices and given universal expression. They are not based on belief, but on experience. Those who practice Huna prove the principles in their own experience.

The author of this very excellent book makes the Huna methods easy and natural, fitting them into their proper Hawaiian setting and yet so smoothly leading you to see how applicable Huna is to your own life here and now. You will find here an impressive array of specific methods and techniques, with clear instructions, which you can use immediately or at any time you need them. I find it particularly encouraging to know that every technique described in this book has been proved by the author in her own experience.

You will find that Huna is a "mystical" practice that you can use every day with full awareness of every part of your being—emotional, rational, and spiritual—and never have to keep secret.

E. Otha Wingo, Ph.D.

Preface

I arrived in Honolulu late at night. It was too dark for first impressions, and so, after the ride from the airport, I checked into my hotel and went right to sleep. The next morning I woke up early and headed for the lanai to see what I could see. From high up in the Rainbow Tower on Waikiki, the view of Diamond Head was magnificent. I was filled with emotion and an overwhelming feeling that I was home.

The business trip in 1980 that brought me to Hawaii for the first time was the start of a new life for me. I knew without being told that beneath the façade of tourist Hawaii lay a deep and rich culture. Back in California, I began a personal study of the history and traditions of Hawaii, reading everything I could find. When I saw a flyer for classes in Hawaiian Huna, I immediately called to inquire about them.

Josephine and Jack Gray taught a series of popular Huna classes in San Francisco based on their training with a teacher in Hawaii and amplified by their own metaphysical work. Like many who are drawn to things spiritual, they had explored other traditions before discovering Huna. (I had at different times in my life delved into Yoga, Tibetan Buddhism, and Orthodox Christianity.) The Grays believed Huna to be an imminently practical form of spirituality—a way to bring mystical ideas into everyday life. They taught it to others with great enthusiasm and dedication for many years.

The Grays' teachings provided a good base of Huna training, and I went on to study with other teachers in Hawaii and on the mainland. I joined Huna Research Inc., the organization created by Max Freedom Long; attended their seminars; and met regularly with a group of Huna students in the San Francisco Bay Area. For several fun-filled years, I was a member of a Hawaiian club that held luaus and hula festivals and provided instruction in Hawaiian language, crafts, chanting, dance, and music.

During this time, I made frequent trips to Hawaii, exploring all the islands. I had always felt especially drawn to the Big Island and eventually bought a house in the Waikoloa area. I became part owner of land near the Puna Cave, a sacred site, and was profoundly affected by this marvel. Since that first fateful trip, Hawaii has never ceased to be my spiritual home, and my love and respect for the Hawaiian people and their amazing culture remain stronger than ever.

My goal in learning Huna has always been to incorporate it into every aspect of my life, so that I reap the benefits of its wisdom. Just as my teachers brought Huna to me, my hope is that this book will bring it to others, with love.

Me ke aloha pumehana,
Charlotte Berney

Introduction

There is a special place on earth, born of lava that has been issuing from an opening in the ocean floor for millions of years. The islands that were created are not like anywhere else on earth. Circled by a limitless sea and sky and adorned by flowering trees and sparkling waterfalls, the exquisite Hawaiian Islands have come to embody an earthly paradise for the rest of the world. They are also the source of one of the world's most powerful teachings.

The body of mystical knowledge known as Huna has its origins in ancient wisdom and an ancient culture, yet is adapted for modern times—and it is completely relevant to these times. The Huna system is rich in insights that are profound and universal and easily understood. It offers practical, hands-on methods that are the fruits of experience. Among Huna's gifts are a personal energy management system and the integration of body, mind, and spirit. Huna teaches us balance in life along with a life-affirming positive approach toward ourselves and others. Huna emphasizes a loving way of life, direct action, and personal responsibility. It gives the practitioner tools to use in virtually every aspect of life.

Huna makes a perfect complement to other spiritual systems and often enhances our understanding of them. No prior knowledge is necessary to study Huna—all that is needed is a simple willingness to learn and practice.

WHAT IS HUNA?

Hawaiian culture evolved in one of the most isolated spots on earth. Hawaiian society included both a powerful religious priesthood and the *kahuna,* experts in various fields who might function as shamans or sorcerers. None of these called what they did "Huna." The term "Huna," meaning "secret" in the Hawaiian language, was adopted by researcher Max Freedom Long (1890–1971) to describe the spiritual and mystical knowledge he gleaned from Hawaiian sources over an extended period of study. Long was well-versed in the new ideas in the fields of psychology and metaphysics developed around the turn of the century, in which the discoveries of Freud and Jung concerning the nature of the mind, and the spiritual tenets of Theosophy put forth by Madame Helena Blavatsky, were prominent. Long was able to recognize a system of knowledge and he described the principles he uncovered in layman's terms through a series of popular books.

Max Freedom Long's Huna has been called a "synthesized system" since it was derived from Hawaiian concepts, and was interpreted by a non-Hawaiian through his own wisdom and knowledge of psychology and metaphysics. Huna is not synonymous with the traditional religious practices of the ancient Hawaiians. The Huna principles that Long gave the world were, in a sense, extracted from their cultural context and given universal expression. Their essence, however, remains Hawaiian, and the Hawaiian source is honored and referenced throughout this book.

Since Long published his seminal works, the word Huna has become a catch-all term for many spiritual practices associated with Hawaii. Other teachers of Hawaiian mystical tradition, both Hawaiian and non-Hawaiian, have emerged to write their own books and offer various kinds of training. Many of these base their work on Long's, while expanding the concepts and adding their own insights. Others mix Huna concepts with their own philosophies and religions. A few of the individuals working in the Hawaiian tradition have contributed greatly to its body of knowledge, and these represent a rich and diverse resource. The teachings of David Kaonohiokala Bray, Josephine and Jack Gray, Allan P. Lewis, E. Otha Wingo, Laura Kealoha Yardley, Serge King, and others will be touched on.

The information given here summarizes collective knowledge about Hawaiian Huna, past and present. It is not presented as a fixed or orthodox system because that is not what Huna is about. Huna does not require belief, but emphasizes the workable and the practical. For that reason it has been called a "science," with the implication that its theories can be proven by experience. There is always room for refinement, and future practitioners will undoubtedly add to this store of knowledge. That is what Max Freedom Long, with his open-minded approach, would have wanted.

THE SECRET SCIENCE

Long chose the Hawaiian word for "secret" to describe this system of knowledge in the sense that it was information kept guarded by the Hawaiian kahuna. There were several good reasons for the knowledge to be kept under wraps. First of all, kahuna knowledge was shared within a circle of practitioners and passed down orally to apprentices, often family members, who were chosen for their interest or their natural ability.

Practices varied widely among the kahuna, and even in traditional times, there were many variations in rituals, words, and prayers. A kahuna's training was derived from his own lineage and traditions, and the kahuna interacted with the gods that were a part of that lineage. Kahuna had their own personal Aumakua, or ancestor gods, that they worked with and who acted as their intermediaries in prayer. For example, the goddess Pele was an Aumakua of Kahuna David K. Bray. He often said of this relationship, "I belong to the fire." Kahuna practices were often passed down through generations of a family and kept intact within the family tradition. Hence there is a lack of uniformity in kahuna practices to the present day, though all kahuna worked then, as they do today, around a core set of beliefs.

After the establishment of Christianity in the Hawaiian islands, kahuna practices were made illegal and were forced underground, and the practices became secret by necessity. Researchers such as Dr. William Tufts Brigham, eminent curator of the Bishop Museum in Honolulu from 1888 to 1918, had difficulty in their attempts to research the kahuna. There was a natural reluctance among Hawaiians to give information to non-Hawaiians who might disapprove, or worse, prosecute. Max Freedom Long encountered this problem in his own research into the kahuna.

Josephine and Jack Gray, Huna teachers in the 1970s–1980s and co-directors of the Institute of Balance, believed that it was best to teach Huna to those who could use it responsibly and were selective in who was taught. The Grays saw Huna as a discipline with its own set of rules and ethics to govern behavior, and recognized that knowledge is power and with power comes responsibility, so they emphasized ethics in all of their training. Just as a physician takes the Hippocratic Oath, the Grays asked their students to take a Huna vow never to influence another person without that person's permission and always to use Huna for the highest good of every being.

Today the consensus is that the knowledge can be shared. One of the first to do this was David Kaonohiokala Bray (1889–1968), a Hawaiian kahuna acknowledged for his life's work by the Hawaii state legislature. He foresaw that kahuna wisdom was in danger of being lost and went to California in the 1960s to teach and train students. Bray established a center in Pasadena for Hawaiian spiritual teachings and also founded a society in Hawaii to preserve Hawaiian language and culture.

Today, Huna teachers give workshops and classes to share their knowledge, and just as in the time of the kahuna of old, the need for personal responsibility in using the knowledge is great. It is generally agreed, however, that secrecy is a thing of the past.

It is also clear that needs have changed with respect to the kahuna. In the past, people who wanted help to change their lives looked to an authority figure to guide them. Today, the emphasis is on self-learning, through books, tapes, the Internet, and other media. Though personal contact with a teacher remains important, people are reaching out today to learn ways to help themselves. With understanding and practice, one can learn to be one's own kahuna, one's own spiritual advisor.

WHY STUDY HUNA?

Huna's concept of the Three Selves and their relationship to one another is of immense help to the individual in achieving personal balance, optimum health, and general well-being. Huna offers a process for dialoguing among the Selves, a means of effective prayer, a method for conflict resolution, and ways of clearing emotional blocks. It allows you to manage your own energy effectively and to direct energy toward your needs and desires. Through Huna you can transform your life and attain a sense of peace within. You can learn to create happiness and success on a daily basis.

Loving yourself, nurturing other beings and the land, and living in harmony with all of life is the essence of Huna. For making personal changes, it is highly effective. Best of all, Huna gives you a definite plan of action. As Max Freedom Long often emphasized, Huna is something that you *do*.

Huna is, as the Huna Research Inc. motto states, "a powerful force in the world." Although Huna enhances life and helps in solving real everyday problems, this book is not intended to address mental illness or to offer medical advice. Problems of this nature require specialists who are trained to deal with them. Those who benefit from Huna are those who are ready to take responsibility for their lives and who have the vision to ascend to a higher level of being.

The Hawaiian Experience

Canoe voyages brought settlers to the Hawaiian Islands from Southern Polynesia as early as 2,000 years ago. A wave of migrations from the Leeward Tahitian Islands followed around 1,000 years later.[1] Those amazing voyagers, who navigated by stars, ocean currents, and other natural phenomena, crossed thousands of miles of open ocean in double-hulled canoes. They carried with them the plants and animals as well as the traditions of ancient and rich Polynesian cultures that developed in the wide area between continents called Oceania. The people who made Hawaii their home evolved a distinct language and culture that retained similarities to other Polynesian groups. The society that emerged was well-organized and complex. A stratified class system, determined by birth, divided the populace into chiefs, priests, skilled professionals, commoners, and slaves. There was a strong priesthood that shared power with the ruling class. A set of laws, the *kapu* (taboo) system, governed various aspects of behavior. Warfare between chiefs and districts for territory and influence was common.

For their livelihood, the people relied on agriculture (the growing of *taro,* sweet potato, and other foods), their domesticated animals (pigs, chickens, dogs), and fishing. They built elegant, sturdy canoes from a hardwood called *koa* and constructed temples, *heiau,* from stone. An artistic aesthetic permeated the ancient Hawaiians' everyday life and was seen in their temple images, elaborate feather work, petroglyphs, carvings of ornaments and fishhooks, and dyed bark cloth. The culture attained a richness in language, poetry, chants, and dance forms.

With the arrival of the British Captain James Cook and his expedition in 1778, Hawaii's isolation ended. Word of the islands soon reached Europe and America. Christian missionaries followed in 1820, and later waves of settlers from China, Japan, Portugal, the United States, England, the Philippines, Polynesia, and elsewhere created a unique mix of races and cultures. Outside influences proved disastrous, however, for ethnic Hawaiians. The Hawaiian population declined rapidly due to introduced diseases from which they had no immunity, while their traditional way of life quickly eroded. Under the edicts of the missionaries, the kahuna could not perform rituals or practice healing. Children went to schools where they were forbidden to speak Hawaiian and were taught English and Christianity. The result was a loss of much traditional knowledge, a decimated populace, and eventual annexation of Hawaii by the United States.

Yet, during this time of drastic change for the Hawaiians,

pockets of the old ways persisted, and the memory of a vital culture remained.

After years of suppression, the Hawaiian language, as well as traditional dance and crafts, began to be revived, along with pride in the culture. Today, a full-fledged cultural renaissance, along with a political sovereignty movement, is in progress in the islands. A new consciousness of the value of all things Hawaiian, from the beauties of language and dance to the wisdom of the kahuna, has taken hold in the place of their origin.

THE KAHUNA

> *Waiho wale kahiko*
> Ancient secrets are now revealed
> (HAWAIIAN PROVERB)

The Hawaiian word kahuna describes the learned classes of old Hawaii and can be translated as "master" or "expert." The kahuna (the same word will be used in this text for both singular and plural) might have been a master of canoemaking, building, genealogy, meteorology, navigation, herbs, medical diagnosis, massage, poetry, prayer, prophecy, or any other specialty found in old Hawaiian society. The term today is most often used to refer to a spiritual master such as a shaman, priest, or sorcerer, which in old Hawaii were only a few of those designated "kahuna." In the old way, the kahuna, who could be male or fe-male, was trained in an apprenticeship system, often with a parent, uncle/aunt, or grandparent, and underwent many years of rigorous training.

The kahuna, as master or expert in a field, was an integral

part of old Hawaiian society, performing many vital functions. For example, the medical kahuna, who practiced diagnosis and healing, was like a family doctor or psychologist who often knew the family well and was consulted for a variety of problems. The kahuna might be called on for simple problems, like cuts, burns, or rashes, as well as serious illness. The kahuna used a wide variety of medicinal herbs, plants, and other natural substances to heal the patient. Unlike current physicians, however, the calling encompassed a great deal more than physical ministration and was more akin to a spiritual intermediary.

The healing kahuna, who acted as a bridge between the spiritual and material worlds, has been the focus of research in recent years. This kahuna approached medical problems holistically, and employed many forms of treatment to cure the patient. The Hawaiians believed that the cause of sickness could come from outside, such as a sorcerer's curse, or from the individual's own action, such as breaking a kapu or offending a god. The sickness could also be caused by a problem in family relationships. The mind-body connection was assumed, with no separation between the problems of the body and the emotions or mind. The medical kahuna first attempted to diagnose the illness, looking both at the physical manifestations and, like a sleuth, searching for the true cause, which was essentially nonphysical. To arrive at the truth, the kahuna observed the body closely for a period of time while looking for any external signs and omens surrounding the patient. Unusual occurrences were noted. The patient was questioned about recent dreams that might prove meaningful, and the family was consulted to provide clues to the cause of the sickness.

Once the origin of the illness was understood and identified, the kahuna used a variety of methods: prayers, rituals, chants, herbs, and massage, to bring about healing. If sorcery were the problem, this could be countered through prayer and ritual. If a god had been offended, some form of recompense could be made. When the problem involved family relationships, a clearing process that involved the entire family, called *ho'oponopono,* was used to identify and dispel the problem. The kahuna often presided at these "family therapy" sessions, which sought to get to the heart of the difficulty and find a solution that worked for everyone. Once the healing work was done, and the patient was on the road to recovery, the kahuna was compensated with food or other goods.

In contrast to this helping role, the sorcerer kahuna used rituals, chants, or poisons, or invoked curses, to harm his intended victim. In old Hawaiian society, the individuals who followed these harmful practices were thought of as renegades and were both feared and avoided. As traditional Hawaiian culture was lost, however, and as the work of the kahuna was suppressed, the word kahuna became more closely identified with the sorcerer. Fueled by misunderstanding, no doubt reinforced, both intentionally and non-intentionally, by the missionaries, this misconception grew over the years. The sorcerer who worked spells and curses in secret to cause illness and death gained a reputation not unlike the witch of the European Middle Ages, while the skillful healer was forgotten.

In recent times, the reputation of Hawaii's ancient kahuna has been somewhat rehabilitated, though misconceptions still exist. Today, with the term "kahuna" applied loosely in Hawaii in such diverse realms as metaphysics and surfing, there is little agreement about what it means, and even the word itself remains controversial. Some say that the kahuna of old were so much a part of traditional Hawaiian culture that no use of the term today is justified. Conversely, there are spiritual teachers working in the Hawaiian tradition who still use the word. This has truly become a matter of individual usage, and the term signifies different things to different people. One alternative is to use the Hawaiian term *kumu*, meaning "teacher" and "source," which also carries the meaning of a respected role model; or to use *kahu*, meaning "guardian."

It is enough to note here that any spiritual leader or teacher, whether called priest, shaman, kahuna, kumu, kahu, or other term, must live up to the name in substance. If the result of the teaching is an enhanced life for the one who seeks the knowledge, then the name is irrelevant.

HAWAIIAN CONCEPTS

Though it is a synthesized system of mystical and spiritual knowledge, Huna is, at its core, Hawaiian. Its basic ideas come out of Hawaiian thought, and while those can be expressed in universal terms, knowledge of their source can provide insights. Therefore, before delving into the specifics of Huna, some understanding (however brief here) of the psychological and cultural terrain of Hawaii will help to enhance its study. Capsule descriptions of concepts that were important to the Hawaiian way of life follow. These are ancient concepts but in many ways they are as alive today as they were in old Hawaii.

Aloha

This lilting word that is known throughout the world evokes a spirit of grace, warmth, and connection between people. Translated as "love," it can mean anything heartfelt from deep personal love to mercy, kindness, compassion, and brotherhood. Used as a greeting, the expression of aloha extends sympathetic feelings and goodwill to create bonds of affection. On a higher plane, aloha is the ideal in human relationships, an empathetic reaching out of a selfless nature, a sharing from the heart in a spirit of generosity and peacefulness. The concept of aloha is the heart of Huna, which teaches that everything in the universe responds to love and kindness. David K. Bray called aloha simply "God in us."

Balance

The concept of balance comes up frequently in Hawaiian thought and is pivotal to it. The English word does not fully describe the Hawaiian idea of pono, in which all is right with the world and all aspects of life are working harmoniously together. For an optimum life, balance was considered necessary, first of all, among the parts of nature—humans, animals, birds, plants, weather, water, land, and sky; among the female and male polarities (the yin and yang of existence); among the gods, demigods, and spirits, greater and lesser, and the humans who interacted with them; and finally, among the members of the extended family, the community, and the various strata of society. The Hawaiian view also held that a healthy life maintained balance between the material and spiritual realms, and these were not considered to be separate from one another. Sex, food, dance, and music were considered spiritual and were integral parts of religion—all were intertwined into a harmonious whole.

To the ancient Hawaiians, behavior that offended a god or violated a kapu could throw the individual or the community or even the natural world into imbalance. To the individual this could mean illness, bad luck, and some form of unhappiness that would shadow the person until balance was restored. To the community it could mean failed crops or some form of natural disaster. When imbalance occurred, the kahuna was consulted in an attempt to find the source. When it was discovered, the kahuna then worked in a holistic way using the elements of nature and spirit to restore healing and harmony.

Breath

The word for breath, *ha,* also means life, and is found again and again in the chants of old Hawaii. Prayer and communication with the gods were associated with the breath of life. In breath was the life force and the individual spirit, considered so elemental that the greeting in old Hawaii was a close face-to-face sharing of the breath of life. When a kahuna was dying, he passed on the power and knowledge that he had acquired in a lifetime by literally breathing it to his protégé. Other Hawaiians passed on their gifts in their professions—their talents and mana—to a family member through their breath. Mana—vital life force—could also be imparted to objects by breathing on them. The use of the breath is at the core of Huna practice.

Dualities

An awareness of dualities runs through Hawaiian thought and poetry, with numerous references to sunlight and darkness, upland and lowland, fire and water. One of Hawaii's oldest literary records, the Hawaiian chant of creation called the Kumulipo, describes life as coming forth in pairs, "man for the narrow stream, woman for the broad stream." These phrases reference, for man, a narrow bay where water flows forcefully, and for woman, a wide shore where the surf rolls in without breaking.[2]

In Polynesian mythology, goddesses and gods duel and love in passionate encounters. The solar deity Maui is often paired with Hina, who resides in the moon, either as wife or mother. In another myth cycle, Hina is paired with Ku, the "expression of the male generating power," while Hina is the "expression of female fecundity and the power of growth and reproduction."[3] In one well-known myth, Pele, the volcano goddess, engages in a colossal battle with her would-be lover, Kamapua'a, the hog god, during which she tries to annihilate him with fiery lava and he tries to quench her fires with ocean waves. Hawaiian mythology also yields the concept that the two energies of the duality must be united and transcended for harmony to occur. As Kahuna David K. Bray once wrote of dualities, "Kahunas are taught about both the positive and negative forces. The positive power works through the spiritual while the negative works through the material. The positive and negative forces have to be together for completeness. All life is the creative union of duality."[4]

Family

The Hawaiian word for family, *ohana,* refers to the extended family, but has a strong spiritual connotation. Today, the term is often used to mean a group of people of like mind and purpose. In old Hawaii, the extended family included not only those related by blood, but also close family friends, those children adopted by family members, the spirits of departed ancestors, and personal guardian spirits. The ohana shared their food and the work to be done, as well as a strong bond of love and mutual protection. In a wider sense, the Hawaiians valued all their relationships—those to their gods, to other people, to plants and animals, to spirits, and to beloved places. These relationships were cherished and held sacred.

Ho'oponopono

On an island chain surrounded by a vast ocean, it was important to learn to resolve difficulties. Though there was often active conflict between chiefs in old Hawaii for control of land and resources, within the family a sophisticated method of conflict resolution was practiced. When a family member became sick or when another kind of problem developed, it was considered that a wrong action or belief might be the cause. An offense to a person or to a god could bring about an imbalance. Once the cause of the disharmony was discovered, it could be cleared away. The Hawaiian practice of hoʻoponopono, meaning "to make things right," was a ritualized process of discovering the problem, airing the grievance, resolving the problem, and restoring harmony.

Kapu

The word originally meant sacred and its meaning was extended to mean forbidden. The latter meaning has entered English and other languages as "taboo." In old Hawaii, the word referred to the elaborate system of laws dictating everyday behavior whose infringements were severely punished. Many of these laws were designed to protect the islands' delicate ecological balance by prohibiting the harvesting and eating of certain foods under specific circumstances. The kapu system also served to maintain the class hierarchies within society. The kapu system was a mainstay of the culture until it was dissolved in the early 1800s. The concept of the sacred and of forbidden or inappropriate behavior remains a strong one in Hawaii.

Love for the land

Aloha aina permeates Hawaiian thought and is found throughout Hawaii's songs and chants. Songs of praise honored beloved places, and the special attributes of the places were named and celebrated. In few other cultures was the spirit of place so deeply acknowledged. This mystical love for the land included within it a recognition of the bond between humans and the earth and the life-giving aspects of the natural world. It expressed a close personal feeling for the land as a spiritual entity.

All land in a sense was sacred, but places of high mana and special sacredness were located on all the islands. Some of these places of power were natural, such as unusual rock formations or waterfalls that were interwoven in Hawaiian legend. The active volcano on the Big Island of Hawaii was, and is, considered to be the living body of Pele and held extremely sacred. The Hawaiians constructed their own sacred sites, the *heiau* or temples, out of stone or wood in the form of platforms situated prominently on ocean shores or hidden away deep in the forests.

Mana

To the Hawaiians, *mana* was vital life force—universal divine spiritual power—that could manifest and become abundant in people, places, or things. The amount of one's mana determined one's success and luck, or lack thereof. It was understood that a person's individual mana could extend beyond the physical body, so that objects owned or handled by a person could be invested with that person's mana. High chiefs were thought to be imbued with especially high mana. A leader like Kamehameha I, for example, was believed to have a powerful store of personal mana, which enabled him to lead and influence others. This is similar to the concept of charisma, in which an individual's overall spirit and energy exert a powerful effect on other people.

In Hawaii, caves, valleys, waterfalls, and other natural features might contain their own special mana. Places could also hold the mana of a person or of a spirit. Natural objects such as gourds, rattles, salt water, and *ti* leaves were used in spiritual practices to impart their own mana, their power.

The kahuna knew how to gather mana and to direct it toward a purpose in order to accomplish specific results. A large part of the study of Huna involves understanding and using this spiritual power.

Names

The *inoa,* or name, was much more than a label to the Hawaiians. It embodied important information about the individual's nature and destiny. The name was considered a living thing that contained power in and of itself. Names determined the course of things. If a given name proved unsuitable for a person, the name could be ritually removed and a new one taken. The importance of names extended to all aspects of the culture, and Hawaiian chants were filled with a multiplicity of names for gods and places. Names were often used by the Hawaiians in symbolic ways: i.e., a certain plant might be used to treat an illness because its name evoked a quality associated with healing.

Nature

The Hawaiians, living close to the drama and power of the elements, did not see themselves as separate from nature. Humans were a part of a natural world in which everything was alive and had its own form of consciousness. There was an exquisite awareness of the natural world in Hawaiian spirituality. For example, a chant in praise of Laka, goddess of the hula, speaks of the rain forest, summit clouds, and summer rains, images fraught with both earthy and spiritual meanings.[5] Chants and poetry weave their stories with metaphors from nature—billowing waves, rain clouds, forest birds, wild boars, great rocks, fruited trees, fragrant flowers.

Elements of nature such as birds, fish, plants, and rocks could also be guardians for the living and were sometimes considered part of the extended family. Special stones were sources of healing, fertility, and mana; fishermen would set special stones on the shore to attract schools of fish to their nets.

Prayer

A belief in the power of prayer permeated the everyday life of the Hawaiians. A Hawaiian saying goes, *"O ka pule ka mea nui"*—Prayer is the most essential thing.[6] Priests recited elaborate official prayers for every occasion, while the common people prayed before felling a tree for a canoe, planting taro, setting out to fish, and in many other mundane circumstances. Prayer is still an important part of life in Hawaii. Few new businesses would open their doors without a blessing ceremony, while events and meetings, from the largest gathering to the smallest, usually begin with prayers. Today, these prayers may be Christian or Hawaiian, yet they follow ancient tradition in affirming the importance of prayer. Prayer is the means by which Huna methods are accomplished.

Spirits

The ancient Hawaiians had a wide array of gods, goddesses, and demigods, as well as family guardians and ancestral spirits to call upon. The concept of a greater god was not emphasized and, when one was acknowledged at all, it was thought to be mostly unknowable and unfathomable by humans. High deities such as Kane, Ku, Hina, Laka, Lono, Kanaloa, and Uli manifested in different guises and in the elements; those like Pele, Kamapua'a, and Maui had complex, human-like personalities.

There was no notion of these deities as inherently good or evil, just as Hawaiian thought did not recognize the dichotomy of good and bad. The closest the ancient Hawaiians came to an idea of evil was "missing the mark," in the sense of not making the right move because of a lack of understanding.

The word *akua* was used in many different ways to refer to various kinds of spirits but it implied both a conscious and an impersonal spirit. *Aumakua* were personal helping spirits from one's own lineage. They could take different forms, called *kino lau,* such as plant, animal, or weather bodies. Spirits of the departed could remain on earth and influence the living or roam as ghosts.

Words

Hawaiians believed in the power of words. With no written language, they perpetuated their collective history and knowledge in chants and a vital oral tradition. Poetry and oratory were revered. The Hawaiian language has compound words and phrases that contain a wealth of nuances and allusion. Words often have double meanings, existing in both the realms of the mundane and the spiritual, the sexual and the divine. These multiple meanings were used with great effect in poetry and chants as well as everyday speech, producing a layered and rich range of expression.

Proverbs and sayings abound in Hawaiian. A Hawaiian proverb that describes the deep respect for the spoken word in the culture goes: *I ka olelo no ke ola, i ka olelo no ka make,* meaning: "In the word is life, in the word, death." Words were thought to have power in and of themselves and to be capable of altering reality. The proper use of words was especially important to the kahuna. When chanting a prayer to the gods, it was believed that the words must be said in the right way or the prayer would not reach its destination. When said properly, the prayer took flight. Words of blessing, prayer, and invocation were part of everyday life in Hawaii.

A GIFT TO THE PRESENT

The ancient Hawaiians valued words, prayer, their gods, the sacred, the breath, a loving spirit, family ties, the elements of nature, and mana—the vital life force. Throughout their culture the goal was to manifest balance, personally and communally. In Huna, these ancient Hawaiian ways of thinking and living have been adapted to our time for use in today's world. Huna is not about going back to the past to re-create a world that is gone forever. Our time is now, and our vibration is of the present. Huna is about a path that can be walked by anyone who takes the time to read, contemplate, and practice. Huna is ancient, but at the same time, magnificently modern.

The Concepts of Huna

Discovering the concepts of Huna is like finding gemstones in a mountain—a joyous journey in which you learn truth and beauty and recover lost parts of yourself in order to become whole again. The ideas are profound, yet elegantly simple and have the feeling of an old wisdom being re-learned.

THE ORIGINS OF HUNA

Max Freedom Long, an American from Los Angeles, arrived in Hawaii in 1917 to take a post as a schoolteacher in an isolated valley on the Big Island of Hawaii. He later moved to Honolulu where he operated a photography shop. While living and working in the islands, he became intrigued by stories of the Hawaiian kahuna—the native priests/shamans—who accomplished what seemed to him to be "magic." He began what was to become a fifty-year study of kahuna practices. Through his research, which included an extensive analysis of the Hawaiian language, he identified basic ideas and practices of the kahuna. He developed these concepts in a series of books beginning with *Recovering the Ancient Magic*. His best-known book, *The Secret Science Behind Miracles,* has been continuously in print since it was first published in 1948.

The word Huna refers to Long's synthesized system of knowledge which he derived from Hawaiian and European sources and set down on paper over fifty years ago. The system includes both ideas and their practical applications. As mentioned, the Hawaiian noun "huna" that he chose to describe this knowledge means a hidden secret; the verb means to hide, conceal, or cover. Long spent years researching and, in his words, "recovering" this system both while living in Hawaii and through his studies of the Hawaiian language after he returned to the mainland in 1931. He believed the ultimate key to recovering the knowledge was in his analysis of the Hawaiian words used for metaphysical concepts—breaking them down into their component parts to search for hidden meanings.

In Long's seminal work, *The Secret Science Behind Miracles*, he began, "This report deals with the discovery of an ancient and secret system of workable magic, which, if we can learn to use it as did the native magicians of Polynesia and North Africa, bids fair to change the world..."[7] In further exploring these concepts, he went on to write other books on Huna, including *The Secret Science at Work, Growing into Light,* and *Self-Suggestion.* In *The Huna Code in Religions,* Long uncovered elements of the Huna system in the world's religions. He founded Huna Research Inc., a worldwide organization that encourages individuals to use the Huna principles and experiment with them, and then share the outcomes. For the rest of his life, Long remained interested in the results others achieved using Huna and in further disseminating the successful ones.

Since Max Freedom Long brought his findings to the world, many other teachers, both Hawaiian and non-Hawaiian, have contributed their own wisdom and experience to the store of Huna knowledge. Though its basic concepts remain the same, Huna is an open-ended system, not an orthodox one. It was meant to be tried and explored, with new insights added to the body of knowledge. As Long wrote, "Huna is not crystallized and set and dead. It is a living, practical system which holds fast to the proven while reaching out eagerly to inspect anything new and promising."[8]

This chapter explains Huna ideas and defines the terms. A note about terminology: though Long deciphered Huna principles by analyzing the Hawaiian language, it is not necessary to use Hawaiian words to practice Huna. Huna is not an esoteric discipline. Rather, the concepts are universal and can be rendered in any language. For the sake of clarity, a few Hawaiian terms for which there are no single English equivalents, such as *mana, aka,* and *kapu* are used in this text. *Ho'oponopono* also is unique to Hawaii. There are other texts available that explore the meanings of the Hawaiian words used to express Huna concepts, though there is not much uniformity in these interpretations. Nonetheless, the study of the Hawaiian language in relation to Huna is a fascinating one and yields many insights into Hawaiian thought and culture. Those wishing to delve deeply into Huna and its Hawaiian sources are encouraged to study the Hawaiian language and especially to listen to Hawaiian chants and songs. Students will discover that Hawaiian is one of the world's most beautiful and expressive languages.

THE THREE SELVES

Max Freedom Long described the Three Selves that make up a human being and the ideal relationship between these Selves. The tripartite nature of the human being has been recognized and called by other names in other systems—Freud's id, ego, and superego; parent, adult, and child; spirit, mind, and body. However, the nature of these component parts and how they can best interact with one another is often either over-complicated or vague. Huna provides a clear, logical description of the Selves and facilitates dialogue among the Selves.

In the Huna system, every individual is made up of three minds (or Selves), the High, Middle, and Low (Basic) Selves. These Three Selves are aspects of the individual and are meant to act as a family. When the Selves perform their proper functions and interact with one another in a balanced and harmonious way, they can create whatever is desired in life. This balance between the Selves is of tremendous importance to the individual's well-being and happiness. If one Self is consistently ignored or suppressed, problems such as illness can result. Often, the desires and agendas of the Selves come into conflict, and that causes dysfunctional behavior. Thus, knowing the attributes of the Selves and how they relate to one another is basic to Huna. The practice of Huna involves bringing these Selves into a working harmony through frequent dialogue.

The words High, Middle, and Low (or Basic) refer to the places in the body where the Selves are experienced and not to a hierarchy of importance. The High Self is generally felt to be above the body, while the Middle Self is experienced in the head, and the Low or Basic Self in the solar plexus. These terms are a convenient way of talking about the Selves, and they do not imply a complete separation. The Selves do mingle and are part of one individual's makeup. However, the Three Selves do have separate domains in which they govern.

Middle Self

The Middle Self, called by Long "the mind that talks," is the conscious, waking, thinking mind that reasons, uses logic, and makes decisions. This talking Self is the most familiar of the three, the one that in most individuals feels like "I." It is experienced in the head, but its energy actually permeates every cell of the body. The Middle Self functions only during waking hours and conducts an ongoing inner monologue of thoughts and words. The Middle Self governs the intellect and sets goals after evaluating what would be best for the individual. Its daily business is to analyze and decree. It takes in sensory information from the body about the outside world and the body itself and makes decisions about behavior based on these data using its own logic, as well as the Basic Self's memories and basic assumptions. The Middle Self can feel love and other emotions to some extent, but tends to operate most often in the realm of logic.

Everyone has experienced the detached quality of the Middle Self's thought. For example, a boy, an inexperienced rider, was thrown from a horse. He described his thoughts as he flew through the air: "I saw very clearly where I had gone wrong and why the horse bucked and why I was now flying through the air. I wondered where I would land, and I hoped I would not break anything and that I would get by with only bruises. Before I landed on the ground, I had already decided I would not let this put me off riding horses, and that I would get back in the saddle as soon as I could and get it right." Thus, the Middle Self was busy thinking and planning, even while the body was flying through the air. This illustrates one of the Middle Self's characteristics: a kind of separation that allows it to stand aside from the emotions, analyze situations, and make logical decisions. This is an extremely valuable component to have in one's makeup. It allows the individual to operate at a level of efficiency undreamed of in the rest of the animal world, where life is approached from the standpoint of instincts, feelings, and basic needs.

In some people, the faculties of the Middle Self are highly developed (scientists, professors, engineers, administrators) and even overdeveloped. When someone describes a colleague by saying, "He's brilliant, but doesn't have good sense," it implies that his Middle Self's logical faculty is superior, but his wisdom and practicality are undeveloped or often not operating. This kind of person is idealized at times in our society, as in *Star Trek*'s Mr. Spock, whose race has evolved to be able to function in the realm of pure logic. It is interesting that on the TV show the other characters acknowledge Spock's superior mind but know this limits his spontaneity and practicality and thus his effectiveness in making decisions.

The Middle Self sometimes does behave as though it is an independent entity from the rest of the body, directing activities and following its own agenda. It seems at times oblivious to the needs of the body or the spirit and often directs the body to do its will. For all its seeming independence, however, the Middle Self's actions are limited by the needs and concerns of the Basic Self (Low Self) that govern the body and the emotions. The boy who was thrown from the horse had a Middle Self who looked upon the situation in a detached way and made the decision to keep riding horses in the future. As he picked himself up from the dusty ground, however, the boy felt far from eager to get back on the horse. He had Basic Self needs that were emotional and physical in nature. He needed time to recover his emotional equilibrium—his self-confidence—and time to let his body's bruises heal. As he limped home, his Basic Self's needs took precedence.

Basic Self

The Basic Self—"the mind that never sleeps"—is the focus of a great deal of attention in Huna practice. This Self is experienced in the solar plexus, but permeates the entire body. The Basic Self, in fact, controls the body: the musculature, the internal organs, the five senses, and the autonomic nervous system. It is the seat of the emotions, memory, instinct, and survival. It governs the immune system and sexual functions. The Basic Self takes in information through the senses and gives the Middle Self data about its immediate environment. It also provides information about the body itself through energy level, heart rate, temperature, pleasure, and pain. It utilizes vital life force or mana to perform all of these functions. The Basic Self generally seeks to serve the Middle Self, but sometimes disagrees and refuses to act in accordance with the Middle Self's wishes.

With a consciousness that has been compared to a child's (sometimes an adolescent's) or an animal's, the Basic Self takes thought and speech (from the Middle Self and other persons) quite literally. It uses a basic form of logic and acts according to its basic assumptions, often ones that were established in early childhood. The Basic Self learns best through repetition and is prone to developing habits. It moves toward pleasure and away from pain. The Basic Self is the mind that feels shame, guilt, and fear, and it can be very secretive, hiding these away from the Middle Self and the High Self. It is oriented toward physical actions and material things and is more impressed by these than by ideas. It communicates best in symbols and pictures. Because of its capacity to experience love, it has sometimes been called the Love Self.

Though some Huna practitioners refer to their "Low Selves," others feel the word "low" has a pejorative connotation that makes it less desirable as a term. For that reason, "Basic

Self" has been used here. Whatever it is called, there is absolutely nothing "lesser" about the Basic Self. Getting to know this powerful part of your makeup and being able to dialogue with it is crucial to the success of the Huna process. To solve the problem of what to call your Basic Self, once you begin dialoguing, you can ask the Basic Self what its actual name is. When you get an answer, you can begin using the Basic Self's name in your Huna work. Once you are on a "first name basis" with your Basic Self, you can dialogue with it as a friend to work out issues and problems. Establishing a loving relationship with your Basic Self and eliminating blocks, faulty basic assumptions, and fears is an extremely important part of the work that you will do.

High Self

Long called the High Self the "utterly trustworthy parental spirit pair," acknowledging its dual nature containing both feminine and masculine polarities. It is sometimes referred to as Father-Mother-God. The High Self is the individual's portion of God, your personal connection to the higher source. The ancient Hawaiians did not look to a higher god overreaching all creation for help and guidance. When they did acknowledge one, they did not feel that this being could be easily accessed on the human level. The High Self, your personal god, is the one who functions, along with your spirit guides, guardians, and angels, to help you through life.

The High Self is the source of insight, inspiration, and absolute love. It can be called upon for healing, for understanding of a situation, for reconciling differences with others, and for connecting joyously with the cosmic realm. For all its powerful nature, the High Self does not interfere with the individual's free will. It is not judgmental and only helps when asked and when it is given sufficient mana to act. It sometimes comes through when you are very relaxed to give you hunches and premonitions. It may intervene when your life is threatened.

Think of the High Self as a transformer between you and the cosmos. The High Self is connected with other evolved spirits—the *Po'e Aumakua* or Great Company of High Selves—which consists of the High Selves of all beings. This company can be called upon for assistance when needed. In day-to-day life, the High Self is always available for help and guidance, as long as communication is not being blocked by harmful assumptions or fears in the Basic Self area. The High Self knows all about you and observes your behavior without condemning. This higher part of you will always tell you the truth when asked and will lead you to the means of help if you request it.

KNOW THY SELVES

To get to know your Three Selves and learn more about their attributes, begin observing your behavior. For example, take the simple act of reading. Your Middle Self may love reading, which feeds the intellect with ideas and information, and it may enjoy reading a wide variety of materials such as newspapers, journals, and nonfiction books. Your Basic Self, however, is probably more selective, preferring material that appeals to the senses and emotional situations, such as colorful magazines and exciting novels. For instance, you may need to read an especially dry textbook for a required class. Full of good intentions, you sit down at night for a lengthy study session, prepared to take notes and ingest information. After ten minutes, however, you feel yourself getting sleepy. Perhaps you make yourself some tea or coffee and continue reading. Suddenly you feel very hungry and head for the refrigerator. After a snack, you return to the book, but by this time, you are less than enthusiastic about it. You decide to put on some music. The music is engaging, and you find yourself closing the book and listening. Finally you decide to tackle the book the next day, and you head for bed.

What you have experienced is a mild and very common conflict between the Middle and Basic Selves. The Middle Self logically decides that the book must be read: it is necessary in order to pass the exam; you must pass the exam to do well in the class; you must pass the class in order to graduate. The Middle Self knows all of this and proceeds to read the book. The Basic Self, however, quickly finds the book boring and not relevant to its needs, so it begins to assert itself: you become sleepy, then hungry, then you crave distraction. Remember that the Basic Self controls body functions. The Basic Self's needs finally usurp the Middle Self's, and the book is abandoned.

Consider another scenario: You decide to read a novel for half an hour before going to sleep. You become immediately engrossed in a mystery story that involves action, intrigue, and romance. The characters become real to you, and you begin to care what happens to them. You feel a bit sleepy but want to read on. You end up reading far into the night when you know it would be more reasonable to get a good night's sleep. For the time being, all thoughts of the next day's work are forgotten. When you go to work bleary-eyed the next morning, you wonder how you ended up staying up so late for "just a book." You have experienced the power of the Basic Self when it becomes excited about something, and again, you have experienced a mild conflict between the Middle and Basic Selves. You have also experienced the special domains and functioning of the two Selves, specifically, the mind of the Middle Self, and the body and emotions of the Basic Self. Essentially, the Self that sleeps—the Middle Self—was kept up by the Self that never sleeps—the Basic Self.

It might be noted that mystery novels are so popular just because they do appeal to both the Middle and Basic Selves. The Basic Self enjoys the sense of danger and the human emotions while the Middle Self keeps busy trying to find clues and figure out "who done it."

Another way of learning about your Middle and Basic Selves is to observe a small child. Children live according to their feelings and move toward pleasure and away from pain. They are happy when their needs have been satisfied and protest when their needs are frustrated. The parent, in the role of the Middle Self, sometimes has to cause discomfort for long-term benefit, such as giving the child a bath, or medicine, or training. Yet the child lives in the present and only knows that the medicine doesn't taste good and the bath is uncomfortable. This illustrates another important difference between the two Selves: though the Basic Self holds all of the memories of everything that has ever happened to the individual, its world is in the present. The Middle Self is the planner who thinks about future consequences.

Where does the High Self come into the picture? In every organization, vision is needed. If you had only workers building parts, and planners deciding how the work should be done, you wouldn't have much of a company. The High Self provides the visionary element, the inspiration, and the higher purpose. It connects you with a higher wisdom and gives your daily life its reason for being. It provides the aspect of creativity to your life.

Consider the work of an artist who decides to paint a picture. The artist has spent years developing hand-eye coordination (functions of the Basic Self) to be able to use a brush like an accomplished artist. She has studied composition, color mixing, and paint application (functions of the Middle Self). She has allocated money and purchased the right paints and brushes at the art supply store (functions involving both the Middle and Basic Selves). She sits down to paint, but what does she paint? She goes into a slightly altered, receptive state and lets images and feelings come (from the High Self). The colors and forms begin to flow onto the canvas through her receptive state as she captures her vision. While she is painting, she utilizes her art training to compose and render her vision. The finished painting shows a successful melding of the Three Selves: the intention and planning of the Middle Self, the technique and learned ability of the Basic Self, and the inspiration and vision of the High Self. She has truly expressed herself since the expression has involved every part of "herself"—in other words, her Three Selves. The Huna ideal is to bring the strengths of all Three Selves together in every human activity to create successful outcomes.

WORKING TOGETHER

The first step for the Huna practitioner is to understand logically (with the Middle Self) the need to work together with the other two Selves. There is evidence of this need all around you. You undoubtedly know someone who is focused in the intellect and always "in the mind" to the detriment of the body and the emotions. This kind of person may appear to act logically, but in fact is only utilizing one part of the equation—the Middle Self. There are also many people who ignore their higher wisdom as well as their logic and pursue physical sensation above all else, in other words, acting mostly from the Basic Self. Those who are excessively focused on material wealth and "things" are also giving their Basic Selves the run of the house. Even holy persons who attempt to "subdue the will" and "deny the body" for a higher purpose, in other words, to live only at the High Self level, are out of balance. None of these modes of operating is desirable or practical in the long run, and eventually, the lack of balance will manifest. After the Middle Self has made the all-important decision to pursue a harmonious balance with the other two Selves, the work begins.

The next step is to learn to communicate with your Basic

Self and gain its cooperation. Most people are unaccustomed to asking questions of their own inner minds and receiving answers but, with practice, a workable dialogue can be reached. In other words, you, as Middle Self, will learn to dialogue with your Basic Self in much the way you would have a conversation between yourself and a child. The "conversation" takes place silently, in a meditative state called the Silence, though with practice you can learn to recognize signals from your Basic Self in your normal waking state. This is not difficult and not really a foreign process. There has always been a kind of recognition that the body is its own entity. People speak of "gut feelings" and "hunches." Massage practitioners even have a saying, "The body knows," to refer to the fact that the body communicates emotional states that the mind ignores or is unaware of. To dialogue in words and pictures is simply taking the communication process a step further. Communication with the High Self comes next, and this is also facilitated by the state called the Silence. Once the lines of communication are open to this higher power, the High Self becomes an inexhaustible source of wisdom and guidance. You can receive information about your health, about loved ones, and about difficult situations. Again, the techniques for accessing the High Self are not difficult to learn and are relaxing and enjoyable.

The Silence provides the setting for the dialogue among the Selves. The very word—silence—signals a going within, a closing off of the world's clutter. All religions and all spiritual disciplines recognize the need and value for silence and an altered state of consciousness. The uses of this altered state vary, however. In Huna, the Silence is a clearing of the mind so that dialogue between the Selves, the gathering of mana, and a prayer-action can take place. The Silence is a receptive state similar to meditation but contains active elements that make it more like a self-guided meditation. In general, it is deeper than contemplation and a lighter state than meditation. With practice, it can be entered quickly and left quickly. While in the Silence, the Selves can come together in a kind of conference call to solve problems.

The key to the relationship between the Three Selves is love, and this cannot be emphasized enough. When a loving, considerate relationship is established between the Selves, and all three feel loved and valued, the individual is on the path toward realizing true potential. Working with the day-to-day emotions of the Basic Self is extremely important. Learning to identify the emotions you are feeling and processing these emotions in appropriate ways is very significant in the Huna system. Using the Middle Self as it was intended—to observe, analyze data, and employ logic—without overstepping its bounds and shutting out information from the Basic Self and High Self is also very necessary for balance. When these two Selves are operating in harmonious ways, the High Self is able to come through and provide wisdom and inspiration. With love as a common thread that weaves the Three Selves together, the Middle Self sets the direction, while the Basic Self manifests, and the High Self provides divine guidance.

1. Three Selves or minds make up each individual personality.

2. The Middle Self is the conscious, waking mind that analyzes and uses logic to guide behavior.

3. The Basic Self governs the body and emotions, holds the memory, and has the mentality of a child or an adolescent, moving toward pleasure and away from pain.

4. The High Self is the Godlike part of Self that inspires you and connects you with your higher purpose.

5. The goals of Huna are communication, cooperation, and love among the Three Selves, so that each may fulfill its role in an optimum way.

6. These goals are facilitated by a dialogue between the Selves that takes place in a meditative state called the Silence.

MANA—THE ESSENCE OF HUNA

When Max Freedom Long visited Dr. William Tufts Brigham at the Bishop Museum in Honolulu to try and learn more about the practices of the kahuna, the learned gentleman advised him to continue his research and to look for a consciousness directing the process, a force, and a substance through which the force could act.[9] Long found the consciousness in the Three Selves and identified mana as the force and aka as the substance. One of the central concepts of Huna is learning how to use this invisible force called mana.

Mana has already been described as spiritual power or vital life force. The traditional Hawaiians, in common with other Polynesians, believed that mana could be strong in certain individuals as well as investing stones, bones, and other objects. Mana is sometimes described as "energy," but the current usage of this word in English does not quite hold the mystical dimension seen as one of mana's aspects by the Hawaiians. They considered the power of a leader to be as much a manifestation of mana as the healing essence in a dose of medicine. A dramatic illustration of personal mana is the laying on of hands by a healer. In this case, the healer transmits mana to the patient to give the body the energy to heal itself. A supply of mana is necessary just to be alive; beyond that, mana is like a rain that nourishes everything it touches. Without its underlying force, things languish and die; with its abundance, things increase and flourish.

Mana is of great importance to Huna because it is the means by which Huna goals are accomplished. The key to manifesting results is the abundance and free flow of mana. Every day of your life, the High Self examines your wishes, hopes, and thoughts, and fashions a future for you using the mana available to it. In order to manifest these goals, the High Self needs a sufficient supply of mana. Where does this supply come from? Mana is gathered and accumulated by the Basic Self and transmitted to the High Self, where it is transformed into outcomes. In order for this to happen, the mana must be able to flow freely from the Basic Self to the High Self. If there is insufficient mana, or if the flow of mana from the Basic Self to the High Self is blocked by harmful basic assumptions, the mana will have difficulty reaching the High Self, or never reach it at all.

Max Freedom Long described the reason for accumulating mana to send to the High Self in his small book, *Mana*. He wrote: "It stands to reason that our High Selves, being spirits without dense physical bodies other than the one shared by the Three Selves of the man, need the force of this denser level of living to work in the denser materials, as in healing."[10] The High Self, then, needs mana in order to work. Having it or not having it determines whether or not your prayers will be answered.

In matters of mana, it is necessary for the Three Selves to work together to gather, accumulate, direct, and utilize it. Those of you who have ever tried to "will" yourselves to a goal (using the Middle Self alone) know the difficulty. Similarly, simply desiring something to happen on an emotional level (with the Basic Self alone) will not necessarily bring it into reality. There may be no mana available to create a new physical reality, and what mana does exist may not be directed toward its intended goal. In Huna, intention and mana work closely together to cause a desired effect. This combination of actions by the Three Selves is described in Huna as a prayer-action.

A Huna prayer-action is more than a prayer in the religious sense (usually thought of as talking to God) and includes elements of the Huna system that are absolutely essential for successful results. The prayer-action is not a ritual in itself, but its elements can be put into ritual format. The basic formula for a prayer-action is this: state your intention clearly (Middle Self); free your Basic Self of hindering beliefs; gather abundant mana (Basic Self); and send this mana to the High Self. If all these conditions have been met, then the prayer will manifest. This is what Max Freedom Long meant when he wrote about "the secret science behind miracles."

Mana is gathered and directed by you on a daily basis. It is accumulated by the Basic Self every day from the air you breathe, the food you eat, and liquids you drink. In the normal cycles of ebb and flow, this mana that is gathered is used by the Basic Self to power the body, and it has to be replenished daily. This is the day-to-day mana you need to think and walk and work. Once your bodily needs have been taken care of, any excess mana the Basic Self has acquired goes toward manifesting (bringing into physical existence) your other needs and goals. This is accomplished at the High Self level. During the course of your life, normal physical and mental activity expend mana. Anything added to this, such as stress (positive or negative) and tension, uses up mana. Emotional turmoil uses up large amounts of mana. Therefore, in order for the Basic Self to be able to gather sufficient mana to run a healthy body and also manifest goals in the physical world, it must be unencumbered by all the things that would deplete mana. These include harmful attitudes, crippling emotions, and excessive physical drains on the body. If the body and mind are being depleted by too much physical or mental stress, mana will be low. This causes goals to manifest very slowly, if at all. Illness and misfortune may also result when mana is chronically low, as germs are allowed to take hold and weakness makes the body "accident-prone."

Blocks to Mana

Mana cannot flow from the Basic Self to the High Self when it is being blocked by a hindering or limiting attitude or basic assumption. Just as the flow of water in a channel is stopped by an obstacle placed in its path, ideas and beliefs can block mana in the human energy system. Take one example: A woman knew her co-worker's birthday was coming up and felt she needed to buy her a present. Though she was extremely busy, she made time to go out shopping. As she left the house, a lot of feelings came up, such as the fact that she had never liked this co-worker and had resentment toward her for things she had done in the past. As she walked around looking in the stores, she realized she was becoming increasingly angry, thinking of the fact that she didn't like her and at the same time felt obligated to spend time and money on her. She finally picked out a scarf, and as she went to pay for it, discovered she had forgotten her wallet.

In this case, the Basic Self clearly sabotaged the Middle Self's intention because of underlying anger and resentment, and "forgot" the wallet. Something similar happens when you attempt to gather and send mana for an intention but have unresolved feelings about it. The Basic Self will not cooperate, and there will be no mana accumulated to flow to the High Self; or, if there is only partial cooperation, the result will come slowly or possibly be distorted in some way.

In the case of the woman who forgot her wallet, some of her

anger and resentment was on a conscious level. When she analyzed the situation, she saw clearly that she had not wanted to buy the present in the first place. It becomes more difficult when the anger or tension or basic assumption is on a very deep level and stems from the distant past, making it harder to recognize.

In another example, a woman decided she wanted to buy a house and needed to acquire money for a down payment. She had a good job but had so far not been able to accumulate enough money to get started. She decided to do a Huna prayer-action to attract the money for a down payment, having no idea where the funds would come from. First, she clearly visualized her goal—a house—and saw herself signing the papers and handing over the check for the down payment. She then generated mana, which she sent to her High Self for the purpose of manifesting a down payment.

After performing the prayer-action ritual several times over a period of some months, nothing had happened to change her financial situation. So, she began to examine her attitudes toward what she was trying to accomplish. In journaling and dialoguing with her High Self, she discovered that she had some deep-seated negative assumptions about money that went back to childhood. Her family had been very poor while she was growing up. In addition, her mother had strong religious beliefs that included the idea that money was evil and "coveting" was wrong. She had often heard her mother say, "Don't want more than you've got. It's a sin." She therefore grew up with the assumption that wanting "more" than your basic necessities was wrong. After identifying this as a belief held by her Basic Self, she realized that it generated guilt feelings whenever she tried to get ahead financially. The Basic Self refused to cooperate in an activity it clearly perceived as "wrong." Using a Huna ritual, she was able to clear this belief and substitute a belief in abundance. As she became firmly established in her new outlook, money began to flow to her. She got a substantial raise at work, and a relative offered to loan her money for the down payment. She was finally able to realize her goal of a house.

Though this woman had done the prayer-action to gather mana to manifest her goal, a belief at her Basic Self level had blocked the mana and kept it from reaching her High Self. The process of Huna, then, is to free the Basic Self of fear, anxiety, negativity, false basic assumptions, and guilt so that mana can be gathered and sent to the High Self to be utilized toward manifesting a goal.

Gathering Mana

You are already gathering mana naturally from air, food, and water. To accumulate greater mana, there are ways of living that enhance mana and techniques you can learn to gather it to you. One of the most effective ways to gather mana is deep breathing done in a ritual manner for that specific purpose. Mana can also be absorbed from the environment: walking near the ocean or a lake, spending time around trees and plants, and hiking in the mountains all put you in touch with powerful sources of natural mana. The vibration of certain sounds helps in gathering mana. Chants generate tremendous mana and some kinds of music have the power to infuse you with mana. Whatever enhances the physical body increases mana. Eating healthy foods and getting exercise on a regular basis are good mana builders. Anyone who meditates knows that it is energy-producing. Simply thinking positive thoughts is a powerful way to contribute to a buildup of mana in the body. Any kind of mental negativity drains mana, while on the physical level, poor diet, drugs, and alcohol interfere with mana.

The goal of the healing kahuna of old Hawaii—as with shamans and healers everywhere—was to acquire and guard personal mana so that it could be used for healing and protection. The kahuna understood the importance of building and conserving their mana, and many of them lived apart from village or family compound in isolated valleys where they spent time chanting and praying. This may be difficult to emulate in today's world, but the principles are the same. Having time alone in silence and being outside in nature are important in order to gather and maintain personal mana. The other aspects of your life are equally important. Having meaningful work to do, enjoying harmonious relationships with those around you, and being of service in some way all help to gather mana.

When you begin to accumulate great mana, what, then, do you do with it? Mana is stored in the body and manifests as physical vigor and a positive mental attitude. Mana that you have acquired can be directed to flow outward for the purposes of healing, work goals, creative projects, or whatever is desired. You can offer mana to a tree that is stressed in some way, to a sick animal, or for world peace. Applying the principles of

Huna integrity, you can use mana to accomplish much good around you.

Other than the body, mana can be stored in certain substances to produce powerful talismans and to use in rituals. Mana can be directed into salt, wood, stones, metals, and oils. For example, salt can be charged with mana and used in rituals or when needed for healing. The wooden carvings of images around Hawaiian temples were charged with mana for protection. Stones that are infused with mana can become powerful helpers. Metal jewelry and amulets can be charged with mana and worn about the body, while objects imbued with mana can be kept in the home or office.

SUMMARY

1. Mana is vital life force, mystical spiritual power, energy.

2. Mana is gathered daily by the Basic Self to power the body and the mind.

3. Mana that is not needed for bodily functions is sent by the Basic Self to the High Self to manifest desires and goals.

4. You can consciously gather mana and direct it to the High Self for whatever purpose you desire.

5. Negativity, as well as mental and physical stress, can deplete mana, while harmful beliefs can block the flow of mana.

6. Successful Huna involves gathering abundant mana and eliminating drains on mana and obstacles to its free passage among the Selves.

SHADOWY BODIES AND AKA CORDS

The word aka means "shadow," "essence," or "shadow spirit" in Hawaiian. This invisible material, which has never been measured by science, is known in other metaphysical schools as "etheric" or "astral" substance. All things—including the Three Selves—and all thoughts have shadowy aka bodies and can form connections via aka substance, which is sticky and elastic. These connections are in the form of cords or threads that reach between things. Aka cords can connect people or can stretch between a person and an object, or a person and a place. These aka cord connections are not limited by material obstacles or by distance, and they can connect persons on different sides of the world. They are the means by which telepathic communication is accomplished.

The aka cords that connect people and things are significant to Huna practice in several ways. Throughout your life, you establish aka cord connections between yourself and people, places, or things. These cords are created whenever you think about someone or something, speak about them, or take some action that involves them. Thus, by thoughts, words, and deeds, you form many aka ties. Thoughts and feelings travel along these slender cords, and Basic Selves communicate with one another through them. How often have you called a friend only to hear that this friend was thinking of you and about to call you? When family members experience one another's illnesses, sometimes over great distances, that is another example of the existence of aka cords and the way in which they connect people at the Basic Self level.

One woman, a student of Huna, reported that her sister became extremely angry at their mother over an incident. Since the angry sister lived some distance away from her mother and felt too upset to want to communicate with her, she did not express her anger or feelings to her mother. That same week, the mother, who had been in good health, fell ill. Sensing a connection, the Huna student urged her sister to process her anger and even though her mother was ill, express it in an appropriate way to her. After the angry sister talked things over with her mother, the mother's illness cleared up as quickly as it had come. Some observers might see this as coincidence, but for students of Huna, there is no coincidence and the strength of feelings flowing along aka cords is all too real.

Over the course of your life, you establish many, many aka connections, and you may have some that are no longer relevant or positive in your life. In order to move on, it is necessary to ritually cut or dissolve those aka cords. Being aware that they exist lets you have more control over your life.

For example, imagine that two men decide to pool their resources and form a small business. In the beginning, all goes harmoniously, and the business prospers. After a few years, however, one partner decides he wants to expand the business and take it in a new direction. His partner doesn't agree, and the two decide to part ways, with one keeping the business. They come to an equitable economic arrangement to dissolve the partnership. At this time, from a Huna point of view, it would be very helpful for the partner leaving the business to ritually cut all of his aka cords to his partner, to the business, and to all of its products. He does this so that both he and his former partner can now make a new beginning. He would also be advised to cut the cords to the physical building where they worked. The two men can still remain friends, yet the aka cords that linked them as business partners have been dissolved.

The kahuna knew that thoughts are things and have substance. A thought vibrating in the conscious mind becomes stronger when it is linked with emotion at the Basic Self level. When a thought is sent into the universe, its aka substance has an effect, however small, but when combined with similar thoughts and emotions and repetitive thoughts, the effect can be great. Thought forms, composed of aka substance, cluster together like grapes on a vine and can accumulate. In this case, like attracts like. Every positive thought you have adds to the store of positivity in the universe, and every negative thought adds to its store of negativity. It is desirable, then, to think only positive thoughts, so that these can cluster together, making your universe a positive place.

SUMMARY

1. All things have shadowy aka bodies.

2. Aka substance is sticky and elastic and not limited by distance.

3. Through thoughts, words, and deeds, you form aka connections with people, places, and things.

4. Thoughts, feelings, and mana travel along the aka cords.

5. It is advisable to cut aka cords if the connections no longer serve you.

6. Thoughts have aka substance and have a material and cumulative effect in the universe.

THE SCIENCE OF PRAYER

Most newcomers to Huna are surprised to find that prayer is Huna's modus operandi, remembering the prayers they learned in their childhood and perhaps still recite in their places of worship. Huna prayer is different and may more accurately be described as a process or a prayer-action. There is a certain scientific aspect to the Huna prayer-action, which has already been introduced in this section.

To reiterate, for this is vitally important, a Huna prayer-action consists of a strongly stated intention that is fueled by free-flowing mana unencumbered by blocks. The prayer can be as simple as asking for harmony in a day-to-day work situation or as complex as asking for a longstanding health problem to be resolved.

Remember that all Three Selves play a role in a Huna prayer-action. The Middle Self, using will and intention, formulates the prayer-request and is in charge of directing the mana. The Basic Self gathers the mana—the raw energy—that is needed and offers it to the High Self. The High Self answers the prayer-request and manifests the desired result. If the prayer-request is for a physical or material outcome, the High Self must have sufficient mana—sometimes a great deal—to manifest a result.

One of the basics of Huna is that mana can only be gathered and sent between the Selves when the Basic Self is cooperative. After all, it is the Basic Self that gathers the mana and delivers it to the High Self. The most desirable scenario in Huna prayer is for all Three Selves to work as one being, doing their part as a team. However, if the Basic Self is conflicted with guilt, shame, fears, and negative self-opinions, the process will be stymied. When these are present, mana will be low, and so no mana will be available to send to the High Self; the Basic Self will feel too ashamed or unworthy to work with the High Self; there will be poor communication between the Selves; and so no prayers will be answered. The prerequisite, then, to effectively practice Huna—and this is crucial to the process—is to clear out blocks and negativity from the Basic Self.

There are a number of effective ways to clear the Basic Self. Forgiveness is number one: asking forgiveness of others you have hurt and forgiving others who have hurt you in a sincere effort. It may also be necessary to make amends in some way. Positive speech is another way of clearing and involves learning to speak positively on a habitual basis as well as, eventually, learning to see the inherently positive nature of things. This is a powerful practice that allows your High Self to come through to you often with help and wisdom. Along with positive speech goes monitoring your thoughts and speech for negative self-opinions and a poor self-image. When these forms of negativity are identified, they can be changed to the positive with wonderful results.

With your increased awareness of self will come a greater understanding of your emotions and a recognition of what pushes your emotional buttons. Then comes learning to recognize your fears and guilts and releasing them. Going even deeper, you identify basic assumptions you have about work, sex, and money, looking at your behaviors in those realms as well as the sources of your attitudes. Ultimately, to clear the Basic Self, you need to identify and dispel deeply held basic assumptions stemming from your early childhood and adolescence. Clearing the Basic Self also involves erasing the effects of past unhappy events or patterns from the recent past as well as events from childhood and even in the realm of past lives. Once all of these have been cleared from the Basic Self, prayer can be activated. If all of this sounds like a difficult task that is too overwhelming, think of it as a process that unfolds as you walk the Huna path. The self-discovery that takes place with Huna is ongoing and involves greater and greater levels of awareness. In looking beneath the surface of your personality, you may encounter problem areas that need to be looked at and healed; on the other hand, you also have the opportunity to discover what makes you unique as a human being and to find unknown strengths and beauties.

Formulation of the prayer is extremely important, and a great deal of care and thought is put into it. A supplicating prayer emphasizes the "lack" of something and is not effective.

Huna prayers need to be worded in a clear, positive way that is in line with the highest good of everyone and everything involved. It is crucial when crafting a prayer to keep in mind the principle never to interfere with another's free will. Visualization can aid prayer by formulating a "prayer-picture" that acts as a blueprint for an ultimate result. For those unable to visualize, holding the thought of the desired goal is just as effective. It is also a good idea to write down your goal on paper. This hastens the process in which the thought takes on physical existence. The best prayer-picture is very straightforward and simple, never complex. When formulating the prayer, it is best not to second-guess the means by which it will become reality. The High Self is very creative and finds ways of manifesting your prayer that you may never dream of.

Breath is the engine that fuels the prayer and gives it life. Everyone has experienced the refreshment that comes when you are tired and you take a few deep breaths. You are momentarily increasing your mana and giving yourself some extra energy. Magnify this process on a conscious level, and you are doing Huna. Deep breathing is one of the main ways to gather mana from the universe, and mana is necessary to make prayers come alive. Therefore, deep breathing is essential to the practice of Huna and is one of the facets that distinguishes Huna prayer from other kinds of prayer. Naturally, the process of breathing is taking place during any prayer. However, what marks the difference in Huna prayer is that deep breathing is done slowly and consciously with the intention to gather mana; then the mana is offered to the High Self for a specific stated purpose. Thus, not only is extra energy or mana gathered with your intention using the breath, it is *directed* mana. The importance of deep breathing and its relationship to energy and altered states is recognized in other systems such as yoga. In Huna, deep breathing is an integral and essential part of practice.

It is important when putting a Huna prayer-action to work to take steps on the physical plane to manifest your prayer. This engages your Selves with the outside world and shows your Basic Self that you are serious about your goal. For example, say you want a job and you create a prayer-action with the goal of employment. It is certainly possible that if you pray successfully, you will receive a job offer. However, remember that the Huna way is to engage all Three Selves and to use every ethical means toward your goal. Updating your resume, calling associates who might know of jobs, and buying an interview outfit in this case would be the equivalent of visiting a doctor and taking medicines when you desire healing. They are stimuli to the Basic Self and signal that you are working toward your goal in every way possible.

The *Ha Rite*, so-named and formulated by Max Freedom Long, is a ritualized form of prayer-action that includes all the elements that make Huna prayer successful: prayer formulation, deep breathing to create mana, visualization, and cooperation among the Three Selves. It is the basic form of Huna prayer-action, and though its setting and trappings may vary according to individual preference, it always has the same basic structure. This process has been likened to "planting a seed" so that a prayer-request can grow to fruition. Following the Ha Rite, the planting can be encouraged by further offerings of mana. It is interesting to note that the kahuna symbol for mana was water, and that mana is often visualized as a "rain of blessings."

Lest you think that the scientific nature of Huna prayer means feelings are not involved, just the opposite is true. Prayer-requests made from the heart with sincere feeling have a greater chance of success. A fervent wish marshals powerful forces in the universe, and if all the other requirements of Huna prayer are met, the prayer will fly to its fulfillment.

SUMMARY

1. The Huna prayer-action is the basis of the Huna process.

2. For prayer to be successful, strong intention and an abundance of free-flowing mana unencumbered by blocks is necessary.

3. It is important for the Basic Self to be free of fear, shame, and guilt.

4. The prayer-request must be rightly formulated.

5. The Ha Rite is a ritualized prayer-action that involves the Three Selves.

CONCLUSION

Max Freedom Long believed that Huna had the power to change the world. His excitement is shared by most people who discover the Huna system for the first time. Usually, this discovery happens by "divine accident," such as the Max Freedom

Long book that fell off the store shelf in front of a person who is now a Huna teacher. What excites people is the chance to combine spirituality with practical techniques that really work and that give them the opportunity to make real changes in their lives.

To reiterate, then, the basic elements of Huna work involve communicating with your High and Basic Selves, using positive speech, clearing blockages and negativity, learning to breathe effectively, gathering abundant mana, and making prayer-actions. All of these practices are straightforward and experiential, and they can be done by any individual. In practice, the concepts really come alive with actual results one can see and feel.

There is, of course, a learning period in which the concepts must be understood and the techniques applied and refined. After a while, practice becomes second nature, and Huna becomes a way of life. Indeed, the knowledge and rituals of Huna are designed to last a lifetime and to provide tools that can be used in a variety of life circumstances. There is more to Huna, however, than just a collection of rules and tools.

What is so special about Huna is that, like other spiritual traditions that have been around for thousands of years, Huna practices flow out of the natural order of things. There is nothing in Huna that is contrived, and no idea or element that does not have a supremely practical purpose in connecting you with your reality. Along with its practicality, there is the aspect of Huna that is most satisfying to students: its recognition of the wholeness of being. Huna acknowledges that all persons contain within themselves a spiritual dimension that is connected to the greater universe, a mind that operates on pure logic, an emotional being with a great capacity to love, and a marvelous physicality—a body of flesh and bones and sensations. Rather than shut any of these aspects of self out of existence by denying them, Huna rather celebrates their existence and integrates them harmoniously into the whole human being's life experience.

The Practice of Huna

After learning the basic truths of the Huna system, the exciting part begins—putting these into practice and watching your life change. The techniques are easy to work with and master. The challenging part is in changing habits and patterns that have not been serving you and are often longstanding. To embark on a path of Huna is to embrace the means of change and to move forward into a new future. Huna is an active, lively science that is essentially something that you *do,* and ultimately, something you incorporate into your very being.

This chapter on practice covers basic ways in which the concepts are put into action. Following the Practice chapter, "Huna for Everyday" (Chapter Four) extends the concepts in many different situations and addresses problems that may come up in everyday life.

Before beginning to practice, there is a vow that is very important for students of Huna to take—that of never affecting another being without permission and always working for the highest good of all beings. This includes non-human beings as well. If people you know are ill and suffering, do not automatically assume that it is the right thing to send healing to them. Always ask their permission or just send mana and let the High Self decide what to do with it. Whenever you are asking for anything for yourself, always consider whether or not it will affect another person. For example, if you want a better position at work, don't ask for someone else's job, but rather that you receive something good for yourself. If you love someone, and this love is not returned, it is not permissible to try to change the other person's feelings using Huna techniques. It is against cosmic law to interfere with another's free will, whether human or animal or any form of life.

The Huna Vow

In practicing Huna, I promise never to use my knowledge or abilities to interfere with another's free will, and I will not use my power to affect others against their will. I will ask permission for the healing work that I do. I respect every being's freedom of choice, and I vow to use Huna for the highest good of every being. I make this promise from the heart, with all sincerity. So be it. It is done.

You are now ready to begin practicing Huna.

THOUGHT FORMS

Thoughts can become things. Every thought begins as a vibration in the conscious mind and becomes stronger when reinforced with emotion. Strong thoughts can manifest in the physical world, and if similar thoughts are held by a large number of people, manifestation is virtually certain.

The late Hawaiian teacher Morrnah N. Simeona saw thought forms in a person's aura as colors, lights, and shapes. She stressed the importance of channeling thought patterns in positive, life-affirming ways. The ever-changing, kaleidoscope-like nature of thoughts that pass through the mind makes them difficult to control, however. An effective way to work with thought patterns is through speech.

POSITIVE SPEECH

If thoughts are things that have substance and effect, then spoken words have even greater power. They are thoughts made manifest in the world. The ancient Hawaiians took the spoken word very seriously, believing in its power to help or harm.

As a student of Huna, the first step in your practice is to work with the Basic Self to begin thinking and speaking positively. This seems to be a simple readjustment, but positive speech is actually a powerful tool to begin programming a positive future. It has been observed that 80 percent of human dialogue is negative, so there is indeed a great need for a positive trend. If you don't believe it, listen to the talk in the office or supermarket. You are likely to hear a constant barrage of talk about things gone wrong or the anticipation that they will go wrong. Some of this negativity has been programmed from an early age, while some of it has come by way of our societies and cultures. Some of it is just plain habit.

Positive speech is such a profound spiritual practice because the Basic Self takes things literally and is always listening to what you say. The cells of your body respond to sound vibrations, and whether they are bombarded by negative or by positive vibrations can make the difference between being sick or well. Anything thought or said repeatedly eventually will be manifested in reality by the Basic Self.

Awareness is the key to positive speech, so begin by listening. Go into a meditative or contemplative state and ask your Basic Self to cooperate with you in speaking positively and ask your High Self to guide you. Then, listen to yourself talk without judgment and without censure. When you hear yourself saying something negative, replace it with a positive statement. If it's too late for that, simply think of what you could have said and move on. When another person says something negative, either counter it with a positive statement or say nothing (don't add anything negative).

One way of keeping on track with this is to form a partnership with another person. When you say something negative, arrange to give that person a dollar. Or, when you hear yourself saying something negative, place a dollar in a box that you later give to charity.

Practicing positive speech is a little like peeling an onion. You discover more and more layers, and finally you understand that this is not a simple practice. What you realize in time is that the human race is so conditioned to perceive pain and misery that most people have formed a habit of seeing it everywhere. In truth, there is nothing negative on earth except in our perception of it. It is not really necessary to view anything as negative, only to observe and understand it. What about the tragedies played out on television, in the community, in individual lives? What about the deaths of children and war and natural disasters that destroy life? Surprisingly, every experience is open to a positive interpretation. Everything that happens is speaking to you about life if you only have ears to listen. Learn to find the "blessing in disguise" in every situation.

There can be confusion when you first start to practice positive speech. Some of the questions that arise are: Am I going to become a Pollyanna? Am I just suppressing my true feelings? How can I express emotions such as anger, frustration, grief? Can I be honest and still be positive?

First of all, there's no downside to being consistently positive. At first it may feel as though you are suppressing your true feelings, but as you practice being positive, this will *become* your true feeling. Second, many people associate anger with negativity, but this is erroneous. Everyone becomes angry at times—it is human—and there is nothing inherently unspiritual or negative about it. There certainly can be negativity in the way anger is processed or expressed. The kahuna knew that to become powerful, they had to understand their emotions and process them in constructive ways. They understood that strong feelings are not necessarily negative—they can be honestly expressed without being destructive.

When you become angry, avoid expletives which give the anger a negative charge and resonate badly in the Basic Self. Don't damn or darn anything, and don't employ expressions using bodily functions to express anger. Remember that words said in fear and anger reverberate in the Basic Self for a very long time. So, what do you say if you should back into another car in the parking lot? Program your expletives in advance to be positive. Use the words of your grandparents that were positive and mild—expressions such as "dear me," "my goodness," "my word," and "gracious me." If those don't appeal to you, find positive alternatives.

Be aware that anything said habitually is a powerful reinforcer. Keep a list of words you use often and habitually—they will give you insight into your basic assumptions. If you often hear yourself saying "good grief" or "no way," know that you are programming your Basic Self with negative expressions. If you often use sarcasm and say, "oh, wonderful" for something you don't like, this is sending a confusing message to the Basic Self. Avoid sarcasm in general.

Note your general speech patterns and how your language is constructed. Whenever you say the word "but," you are implying a situation of conflict. Substitute "and" and it becomes a statement of facts. Pay attention whenever you hear yourself saying "try" and "should." "I will try" often means "I don't want to, but I don't want to say so." "Should" often implies heavy conflict or guilt. The word "should" frequently points to a conflict between the Middle Self and the Basic Self.

One note: when learning to practice positive speech, be careful not to make yourself feel guilty about saying something negative. Just look at what you are saying and question—what does it mean to you? What else could you have said? Change it to the positive. Keep your general goal of positive speech in mind, and the Basic Self will gradually get in the habit of speaking positively.

Be wary of exaggeration, which in some persons can become a habit that gets out of hand. Those who exaggerate generally want to make themselves more interesting or exciting, but this is really a mild form of lying. Listen to yourself when you describe a situation. Are you embellishing? Ask your Basic Self to stick to the facts. Avoid word inflation—using words such as "great" or "fantastic" when you don't really mean them. That is another form of exaggeration. Use the words "very" and "really" only when they apply.

Contradiction is another bad habit of speech that resonates badly in the Basic Self. You all know someone who always counters any statement you make with the opposite. This can become a habit that creates dissension and distrust among people. It is never constructive. Listen to your interaction with others. If you are constantly disagreeing, ask yourself why. Is it out of habit? When you sincerely have another perspective, simply state your idea as another point of view. Arguing or disagreeing seldom changes another's viewpoint and usually only serves to harden it. How do you handle it when someone else is constantly contradicting you? Let it go, and see that person as a "teacher" by reverse example.

Avoid asking "really?" as a matter of habit in a conversation, unless you are questioning the veracity of what you are hearing. Be aware that when you say "I know," you are expressing to the other that you have the same understanding. Repeating "you know" often means that you are having trouble communicating.

Thanks and gratitude are powerful ways of speaking positively and raise mana in both the one who thanks and the recipient. When gratitude comes from the heart and is sincerely expressed, it reinforces positive outcomes and sets up a strong positive vibration for the future. Thanking the universe and being grateful for the beauty and goodness around you predispose you to more beauty and goodness to come.

When it comes to psychic protection, positive speaking is one of the best ways to strengthen the Basic Self and protect it from psychic suggestion or even attack by others, whether the entities are in the body or out. Habitual negativity drains energy and thus opens up the aura to invasion. As you clear out harmful patterns from the Basic Self, you create a strong and healthy mind that resists any form of possession.

In general, then, when you are learning to practice positive speech, listen to yourself as much as you can and gently guide your verbal expression to the positive. Be watchful of anything said with emotion and anything said habitually. Remember that words are things. In this way, your Basic Self will form the habit of speaking—and thinking—positively. This will make a world of difference in your life.

POSITIVE SELF-IMAGE

The Basic Self's memory banks are the repository for all the thoughts, opinions, and judgments you have ever heard, beginning in the womb and accumulated during a lifetime. Teachers, classmates, friends, parents, siblings, and later, spouses and co-workers, add to the stores. Often these judgments are negative, and are believed and held in the Basic Self. Add to this the judgments and pronouncements of a society, and this can amount to a heavy burden of negativity carried by the Basic Self.

When students of Huna are asked to monitor their negative thoughts about themselves, most are shocked at the sheer volume of them. The criticism you heap upon yourself may begin with that first morning look in the mirror and end with that last thought at night about the "things I should have done." It is no wonder the Basic Self often feels angry, frustrated, and depressed—it frequently is made to feel "not good enough," "not beautiful," "not competent," "not successful," and "not strong."

Just as you monitor yourself for negative speech, begin—and this is a far more subtle task—to observe how often you think negative thoughts about yourself. Catch yourself when you are looking at your body and judging it to be flabby, overweight, or unattractive in some way. Notice when you are given a compliment how you often disbelieve it and decide the giver must be insincere. Observe how you drive yourself to do too many things and then berate yourself for not measuring up. When your work doesn't go well, notice how you find yourself thinking that it's your fault. See how you react when you watch a beautiful actress or handsome actor in a movie or see an elegant fashion model. Do you have feelings of inferiority? When you observe an obviously wealthy, powerful, or very successful person, do you feel insignificant or inadequate?

A great deal is said in our society about the importance of self-esteem—with good reason. From a Huna point of view, a lack of it is crippling to the Basic Self. When the Basic Self is burdened by a negative self-image, communication with the High Self is blocked or hindered, and mana is low. There will be little mana to flow to the High Self, so prayers will be answered slowly, if at all. Therefore, it is critical to build a good self-image, no matter where the negative data came from in the past.

Once you begin to notice how many negative thoughts you have about yourself, you can start to change this. Program a positive self-image into your daily life. When you look in the mirror, see yourself as a marvelous being crafted by God, a precious and unique bit of matter in the universe. Appreciate yourself for and by yourself, without any other frame of reference. Form the habit of being nonjudgmental about yourself (and others) and instead foster understanding. If you feel that your work could be better, really look at the situation. Have you set standards that are too high? Is something preventing you from working to your full capacity? Do you have a fear of failure? If your body is not to your liking, ask yourself if you are truly unhealthy or trying to live up to an impossible image. Cultivate a loving, thoughtful attitude toward yourself rather than a critical one. Forgive yourself frequently.

Sincere praise is always welcomed by the Basic Self and has magical results. When you have done something well, let yourself feel a sense of happiness and satisfaction. Praise your Basic Self for successes in its special domains of health, feelings, and memory. Make your Basic Self feel valued and loved. The result will be a Basic Self capable of taking its rightful place in the trinity of Selves and functioning in an optimal way to create health, energy, and a joyous sense of living.

Once you begin developing a more positive view of yourself, you will find your sincere praise extending to other people. Sincere praise for the good in others raises everyone's vibrations.

Practice positive speech and a positive self-image for two weeks, making a serious effort to pay attention to your thoughts and words. It is helpful to keep a notebook in which you list your habitual expressions and thoughts. Putting them on paper gets them out of your mind and speech so you can become aware of them. Spend time with a mirror to form a habit of body appreciation. Begin to love your body—all of its cells and contours and facets. Let everything go that you've ever learned or thought about your body and see your extraordinary beauty, inside and out. Finally, practice loving yourself the way you would a child—completely and constructively—with their highest good in mind.

These practices set the stage for communicating with the Basic and High Selves. Once you are feeling a new positive outlook emanating from your Basic Self, you are ready to go into the Silence and begin dialoguing with your Selves.

DIALOGUING AND THE SILENCE

The Silence is an altered state similar to meditation, yet it does not involve the deep states associated with meditation practice. Unlike meditation, which is usually described as a deep communion with the divine, the Silence is a lighter form of trance state where communication takes place between the Three Selves using words, symbols, or pictures. The Silence begins with relaxation and quiet in a safe, comfortable place. Use whatever process you need to become quiet, relaxed, and contemplative. Heavy foods, alcohol, and drugs are not conducive to this state. Relaxation techniques that lessen tension in the body are helpful. Put your mind in a state of peace by letting go of thoughts of work, family, politics, and all the daily concerns. Give yourself the time and space to be alone without interruption. A designated space in your home where you can close the door is ideal.

There are no hard and fast rules about the Silence. It can be entered in many different settings and times. Focusing on the highway while driving at night produces a kind of altered state, but it is not advisable under any circumstances to enter the Silence while driving a car. Learn what works best for you to enter the state. You may want to create a place in your home with an altar where you can light a candle. When you have a special place for going into the Silence and use a bit of ritual, like music, incense, and a candle, your Basic Self will soon know exactly what to do when you enter that space. If you choose to enter the Silence outdoors, find a place where your Basic Self will feel comfortable and safe.

For first-time meditators, it is helpful to do a relaxation procedure at the beginning of your session. Sit in a comfortable chair in which you can keep your back erect and both feet on the floor. Remain quiet, with your eyes closed, and, beginning with your feet, consciously relax each part of your body. Bring your attention there, and say, "I am now relaxing my feet. I am letting go of every bit of tension in my feet. I am now relaxing my feet." Then, when you feel your feet relaxing, continue: "I am now relaxing my legs," and so on, until every part of your body has been consciously relaxed. When you have finished relaxing your body, sit with your hands clasped in your lap, both feet on the floor, and focus your attention on a spot on your forehead, between and a little above your eyes. Hold your attention there.

With your eyes still closed, empty your mind of thoughts, and take four slow, deep breaths, exhaling slowly through pursed lips. Continue to breathe slowly, and be aware of your breath. When thoughts come to your mind, gently dismiss them and bring yourself back to a place of emptiness. Take several more sets of four slow, deep breaths until you have entered a state of calm receptivity.

Some practitioners find it helpful to count slowly from one to five and with each number enter deeper into the Silence. By the count of five, they are fully in the Silence. Though people experience the Silence differently, the body is always in a resting state, while the mind has let go of active thinking. If you go too deep into this state, you will fall asleep. After repeated practice, you will learn to go into a meditative state between conscious mental activity and sleep. When you are truly in the

Silence, you will have a sense of being somewhat detached from sensory input: temperature and sounds will still register but in a different way. Your body and mind will both feel at rest.

When you want to come out of the Silence, simply count from five to one and then open your eyes. (Before going into the Silence, give yourself the general suggestion that you will feel awake and fully alert when you reach the count of one.) It would be good to practice going in and out of the Silence on several different occasions until you are comfortable with this state before beginning to dialogue with your High and Basic Selves.

Your goal is to quiet the "mind that talks"—the Middle Self—so that communication with the other Selves can take place. Your Middle Self has a tendency to run off on verbal tangents. When this happens, simply return to the place in your mind that you have established as a quiet zone. Invite your Basic Self to be present and to speak with you. Listen for an inner voice (not an audible one), that seems to emanate from the area of the solar plexus. Your Basic Self may be reluctant to speak to you at first. Be patient and loving and encourage it as you would a child.

Some people experience their Basic Selves as children, some as adolescents, and as male or female. Many people experience their Basic Selves as being the same gender that they are. This does not have to be the case, however. Don't characterize your Basic Self ahead of time, rather let it be whatever it is. The Basic Self, of course, is not an "it," but that word is used here since the gender is not known. The Basic Self may give you a name and if so, you may address it by name when dialoguing.

Once you have entered the Silence, invite your Basic Self to tell you what it is feeling—without interruption from the talking mind. Your initial words might go something like this: "My dearest Basic Self, I wish to communicate with you and to hear your voice. I will be silent and I invite you to speak for as long as you wish. I love you." This can be said silently or audibly. The Middle Self then clears out all thoughts and waits. Perhaps you will not get a response at first. Try it again at a later time. One reason you may not receive a response is that your Basic Self may be upset or angry with you (the Middle Self), and just as a child or adolescent goes into a room and locks the door, the Basic Self may withhold words. With loving persistence, however, the Basic Self will begin to communicate.

When dialoguing with the Basic Self, remember the ways of a loving parent who knows that love works more wonders than harshness. See the Basic Self as a cherished part of your makeup—one of the keys to creating personal harmony and wellness. Treat the Basic Self with respect, love, and caring. As your Basic Self begins to communicate with you and your relationship grows, both your Middle and Basic Selves will be more comfortable in this dialogue. Many people have found that using a pendulum facilitates the process.

Once you have established contact with your Basic Self, you can ask questions and receive answers. This dialogue is crucial to understanding manifestations in the body. The body is an amazing instrument with endlessly inventive means of expression. The Basic Self can turn an unexpressed feeling of anger into a headache, a feeling of resistance into fatigue, and even longstanding resentments into cancer. When the Basic Self cannot communicate in any other way, it uses the body to send a signal about its feelings. That is why it is of utmost important to dialogue with the Basic Self and reach an understanding on a regular basis—before the need for expression in the body. Once a situation has been created in the body, the Middle Self can ask the Basic Self to provide information about it and to participate in resolution and healing. Cooperation between the Basic and Middle Selves is essential.

One of the best ways to accomplish any of your goals is to forge a bond between the Middle and Basic Selves and to reach an agreement about a suggested course of action. Frequently, the Basic Self and the Middle Self have different and often conflicting agendas. For example, your Middle Self may wish to learn a new language, but the Basic Self finds this study tedious and even threatening. Your Middle Self may want to lose weight for health and beauty reasons, but the Basic Self doesn't want to give up desserts and snacks. The Basic Self loves painting pictures, while the Middle Self finds it a waste of time. All of these are conflicts that have to be resolved by agreement between the Selves. If the Middle Self forces the Basic Self to do something such as learn a language (which involves memory) without agreement, the Basic Self will sabotage the work. A diet will go much better if the Middle Self does its homework by dialoguing with the Basic Self about the real need for the changes in eating habits. Making time for activities the Basic Self enjoys, such as music, art, and sports, is a good way of showing the Basic Self that the Middle Self respects its concerns. Dialoguing and reaching agreement on relatively minor issues sets the stage for cooperation over more complex problems.

Communicating with the High Self is the next step for the student, and this can be an enlightening, joyous experience. Go through the body relaxation procedure as above, with eyes closed, hands clasped in your lap, and both feet on the floor. Focus your attention on the spot on your forehead and go into the Silence. Take several sets of four slow, deep breaths, blowing the air out softly through pursed lips. Clear the mind and enter a state of quiet receptivity in which all thoughts are gently laid aside. Then, ask the High Self to come down into the body and to be completely present within you. You will likely feel a gentle warmth and a surge of energy, or you may just feel a quiet sense of presence. Sometimes the High Self will announce its presence by saying simply, "I am here." Again, this is an internal voice experienced as different from the Basic Self and the everyday talking mind. It is never an audible voice.

While in the Silence, you may feel other unfamiliar sensations such as heat, tingling, and a rocking motion. You may also feel an urge to sleep. After a while, you will find the right state for dialoguing. Generally this is a light form of meditation in which you are consciously receptive while remaining in a mildly altered state.

The High Self is your source of wisdom and guidance, your connection with the infinite. This self is experienced as a loving friend, a benevolent parent, and your personal "guru." What students of Huna know is that the Basic Self will block access to the High Self if the Basic Self is feeling unworthy, ashamed, or conflicted. As a being of peace and harmony, the High Self is reluctant to enter a place of discord. Establishing a working relationship with your Basic Self first is the best way of assuring that you can dialogue with the High Self. It also assures that you will be able to gather the mana you need at the Basic Self level to send to the High Self. Once in contact with your High Self, you are free to ask questions and request advice, just as you would of a teacher or counselor. The answers you receive often will "feel right" to you and affirm your inner wisdom. As you become more adept at communicating with the High Self, you will be able to get whispers and glimpses from the High Self during your day-to-day life that will come to you in the small silences when your mind is calm and your body relaxed. The High Self will never interfere with your free will. If you allow yourself to be open and to ask for guidance, then it will come to you as often as you need it. The High Self literally will answer your prayers.

After you have made contact with the High Self on several occasions, go into the Silence and ask the High Self what you can do for it. Listen for an answer. It will most certainly be something that benefits you. When you feel lots of trouble around you, ask the High Self to come to you and take full charge of your affairs, bringing to you whatever you need to evolve. If you have a hard task to perform, ask the High Self to assist you. If you are upset, ask the High Self to restore your balance. If you have to deal with a difficult person, ask the High

Self to help you deal with the situation. When you need healing for yourself or someone else, request it. You will know when you are getting answers from the High Self because they are serious, usually short, and very authoritative in tone. After a while, you will know whether the answers are coming from the High Self or Basic Self. If the answers come very slowly, they are not from the Basic Self, but from the Middle Self. The experience of Huna practitioners is that both the Basic Self and High Self answer quickly.

Over time, you can condition yourself to go into and out of the Silence quickly. Give yourself a suggestion to do this, such as "When I take four slow, deep breaths and then count slowly from one to five, I will enter the Silence. When I count from five to one, I will come out of the Silence." In that way, you can get answers to questions and stay in frequent contact with your Selves. As you communicate with the High Self and Basic Self on a daily basis, it will become easier and more natural. You may also find that your Basic Self will "bring up" information about problems that you need to work on, while the High Self will send you the means of help and moments of divine inspiration.

GUIDES, GUARDIANS, AND ANGELS

Your High Self is your personal link to God/Goddess and the higher realms and is always available to you for help. There are other cosmic beings who assist those in physical bodies, and you can call on them for special kinds of help. Your guides are those beings in spirit form who take a special interest in you and whose wisdom can be accessed on a personal level. During the Silence, you may make contact with such a spirit guide, learn its name, and communicate with it often. Guardians are spirit beings who look after your welfare and exercise a protective role in your life. In old Hawaii, guides and guardians often took the form of deceased relatives, totem animals, and elements of nature. Gods and goddesses may also function as guides or guardians to you.

Angels are highly evolved beings who perform nurturing roles on a cosmic level. They often appear spontaneously when needed but their help can also be requested. Archangel Michael, a universal being, is a special helper to students of Huna and can be called on for help in difficult situations.

As you begin to spend more time in the Silence and to work with your own Higher Self, you make yourself open to the benevolent effects of your guides, guardians, and angels on a daily basis. The Poʻe Aumakua, or Great Company of High Selves, can be called on for assistance when the request is for larger societal or global changes.

ELIMINATING BLOCKS

The obstacles you are likely to encounter in this process of dialoguing with your High Self in the Silence come from your fears and harmful basic assumptions. The kahuna compared these to knots in a cord that prevented the free flow of energy along the cord. These knotty problems can originate from a variety of sources: from childhood, from a past trauma, from your training or education, and even from past lives. They encompass everything from embarrassing incidences to mindless terrors.

They often take the form of faulty basic assumptions and severely limiting beliefs. Everyone has been exposed to these obstacle-creating experiences in their lives. Huna offers techniques to begin to undo the knots and release them.

Forgiveness

As with every Huna practice, you start off simply and advance to the more complex. One way to begin eliminating blocks is to make amends and seek forgiveness for all the hurt you have ever done in your life. Sit down and make a list of all the people you have hurt in the past. If they are still alive, ask their forgiveness in person or in a letter. If appropriate, make amends on the material level with a gift or some form of recompense. If the persons have passed on, go into the Silence and ask for forgiveness in ritual fashion, then make a gift of goods or money to a relevant charity in their names. For example, many people feel guilty for something they did or did not do for one or both of their parents while they were alive. Go into the Silence and ask the parent's forgiveness. The next day, give a donation to the parent's favorite charity in his or her name.

A forgiveness dialogue might go like this: "My dear one, I don't know all the pain and hurt you experienced that involved me, but I know that I sincerely regret it. I did not have the awareness I have now. Today, in the presence of the Basic Self and High Self and my guides, angels, and guardians, I ask for forgiveness and to make amends. I am truly sorry for your hurt and the ways in which I participated in it, and I sincerely ask your forgiveness. I am letting go of all my guilt and shame that

I had because of this hurt to you. Let us both ascend to a place of light and walk our paths in peace. Let us both be released. So be it. It is done."

Spend time with this and do it with sincerity and a heartfelt desire to receive forgiveness for what you have done. Ask forgiveness of each person one at a time, in separate sessions (perhaps on succeeding nights) until you have asked and received forgiveness from all of those you believe you have hurt. At the end, do a general ritual in which you ask forgiveness of all the people you have ever hurt in your life, including yourself, by thought, word, or deed, both known and unknown to you, throughout all time. Ask that you all be released from the hurt and the guilt, and ascend to a place of light.

The next step is to make a list of all the people who have hurt you. Write out a description of the hurts that caused you pain in the past and the people associated with them. See if you can understand what was really going on. How were they mirroring you and vice versa? Did you contribute to being hurt? See the hurt in perspective. Then, if possible, contact the person and forgive them face to face, by telephone, or in a letter. If this is not possible, do the ritual at home for each individual.

Go into the Silence, with a picture of the person nearby if possible. Imagine them sitting there with you. Ask both the Basic Self and the High Self to be present, as well as your guides, angels, and guardians. Explain to the person, as though they were sitting beside you, about the hurt you suffered, and address them in this way: "My dear one, you will probably never know all of the pain and hurt I suffered that involved you.

You did not have this teaching, and we are all learning and evolving. With this awareness, and in the presence of the Basic Self and the High Self, and my guides, angels, and guardians, I fully and sincerely forgive you for my hurt and suffering. I acknowledge my feelings of anger and resentment and release these emotions to the universe to be transmuted to a higher vibration. I truly forgive you. We are now at peace. Let us ascend to a place of light. So be it. It is done."

As with those you have hurt, do a general ritual for all of those who have hurt you, by thought, word, or deed, both known and unknown to you, throughout all time. Ask that you all ascend to a place of light and be released.

In doing these rituals, it may be necessary to go beyond individuals and forgive whole races of people for hurts to you or by you. For example, if you are Jewish, you may want to forgive all Germans; if Native American or African-American, all white people. If you feel guilty about the wrongs done to a group of people by your own group (even if you personally did not participate in the wrongs), you may want to ritually ask forgiveness of the entire group. Group guilt and group victimhood can cause your Basic Self to feel unworthy and ashamed. Hurts and hatred can go back a long way and be part of your lineage and even your cellular makeup. But even these can be released.

Know that when you are asking for forgiveness and forgiving others, you are not erasing the past or your memories of it. What you are erasing is your Basic Self's load of negativity, which can only cause you harm and dysfunction. Stored anger, hatred, shame, and guilt rankle in the soul and become toxic. No matter what the acts of the past were or how badly they affected you, the only health-giving way is to sincerely forgive, be forgiven, and move on.

Changing Basic Assumptions

Once you have forgiven and been forgiven for past hurts and wrongs, your Basic Self will carry less of a burden. You still, however, may be burdened by harmful assumptions that you have carried around since childhood. For example, a girl who as a child was made to feel less worthy than a brother because she was "just a girl" will carry a sense of "lesser than" into adulthood. She may be unable to function in capacities that call for authority and decision-making. A child whose mother abandoned him may distrust women in later life and always fear that, when he loves them, they will leave him. These are beliefs that adhere to the Basic Self and govern future actions in an unwanted way. To function optimally, these erroneous basic assumptions must be changed.

Sometimes it is difficult to discover just what your basic assumptions are, just because they are so "basic." You can't see the forest for the trees; in other words, you can't see the overall picture because you are immersed in it. When an assumption involves something perceived by the Basic Self as shameful, such as "My sexual needs are dirty," it may be hidden away from the light of everyday thought. It continues to operate, however, and to cause unwanted behavior.

Keeping a journal is a very good way of discovering your basic patterns. When a daily problem arises, and strong emotion

94

is felt around it, write down your thoughts and feelings about the situation. This helps to clarify your thoughts and feelings and acts as a record so that, over time, patterns can be discerned. Once you discover the pattern, this becomes your key to working on changing or releasing it. Another way of discovering your basic assumptions is to work with a trained hypnotherapist. In the hypnotic state, with the Middle Self silent, the hypnotherapist communicates directly with the Basic Self to discover deeply held thought patterns. Once these become conscious, the hypnotherapist can guide the Basic Self toward a new awareness. Psychotherapy, counseling, and other forms of "talking cures" can help you recognize your basic assumptions and change them.

A little known but very effective way of discovering your patterns and clearing out harmful basic assumptions from the Basic Self is the Vector method. The Vector method was developed by George Woolson Burtt (1914–1984) and is practiced by certified Vector counselors such as Ben Keller and John Bainbridge, the latter an expert and author on Huna. In the Vector method, using a guided conversation between the counselor and the person needing help, the thought pattern that is causing the problem is identified, as well as the emotions that accompany it and the mental or physical stress caused by it. Once these are truly understood, they are quickly dispelled using the Vector technique. The process is not a lengthy one and may only require one or two sessions. John Bainbridge explains the Vector process and shows how it complements Huna in his excellent book *Huna Magic*.[11]

In Bainbridge's text, he uses the term "complex" in the Jungian sense of a group of related feelings and thoughts that have clustered around a nucleus of experience. According to the Vector method, a complex contains four aspects: an erroneous basic assumption, a specific emotion surrounding the assumption, some form of mental or physical stress around it, and finally, an "always" or "never" way of storing the memory. You begin by identifying a problem that you have, which is currently an obstacle to your happiness. The search then begins for the thought pattern behind the problem. Since many basic assumptions begin very early in life, it is helpful to recall the first incident when the problem arose. This, according to Bainbridge, can be accomplished on the conscious level—when the Basic Self is asked to produce the memory, it does so. Once that memory is found, the emotion, the stress, and the always/never aspect are identified. After these have been discussed and understood, the basic assumption can be released and the complex eliminated. The Vector counselor always works with the client's own belief system rather than imposing a framework. It is important, says Bainbridge, to keep the process simple and straightforward.

An example of the Vector process at work is the case of a woman who was having a vision problem. She had been diagnosed with the same visual problem as her mother, but the problem was not considered hereditary. The student became increasingly concerned because both her eyesight and her mother's worsened over a period of time. Both had been seen by eye specialists and were told there was no way to prevent or alleviate the problem. The daughter was a student of Huna and felt that she was creating a problem like her mother's on the Basic Self level, but she could not discern the reason. She consulted a Vector specialist to get to the basic pattern.

The Vector counselor asked the woman to revisit her childhood to find a time when she wanted to be like her mother. In the Vector conversation the woman discovered that when she was forming her concept of self, she began emulating a powerful and positive role model—her mother. The basic assumption was, in childhood, "I want to be like my mother." The emotion surrounding this assumption was a natural one at first, and later, was based on love and admiration. As the student looked at the course of her life, she saw that she had emulated her mother in many ways, and much of that had been positive. Once a powerful basic assumption is operating, however, the Basic Self does not distinguish between positive and negative results. Developing the same vision problem as her mother had obviously come from the basic assumption, "I want to be like my mother," but in this case, it was undesirable. The mental and physical stress caused by this assumption arose when, in emulating her mother, she created a disease that affected her health and happiness. The always/never aspect was an "always"— her Basic Self believed she should "always" be like her mother.

Once the complex had been discovered and analyzed in this way, the Vector counselor helped the woman dissolve it by helping her identify where in the body the specific emotion was stored. She stated her intention to release it. He then assisted her in ritually pulling it out of her body and throwing it into a symbolic fire. With the emotion went the basic assumption, the stress, and the "always" aspect. The Basic Self was then freed of it. In the woman's case, the effect of the Vector session was noticeable when, over a period of several months, her vision improved and continued to improve.

The kahuna knew that emotions are powerful indicators of belief systems, conflicts, and fears. Noticing when you feel emotion and what "pushes your buttons" is extremely helpful in learning about your patterns. On any given day, you may be given the key to understanding your difficulties. Your basic assumptions are hidden in the emotions you express on a daily basis, if only you pay attention to them. Observe what makes you angry, sad, excited, and happy. Write these feelings down in your journal, and patterns will soon emerge. This may sound like a lot of "homework," but it takes relatively little time using this method for you to be able to see your own issues clearly. For example, in the workplace, you might find yourself reacting with emotion every time something or someone suggests that you aren't doing a good job. Look more closely at this. Was there a critical parent who gave you the feeling you "weren't good enough"? Is your Basic Self still reacting to this critical parent? Look honestly at your emotions for a key to unlock your basic assumptions.

When it comes to issues, you might try dividing your notebook into three categories: work, love/sex, and money. It is safe to say that most of us are carrying around an erroneous basic assumption in one or more of these categories. For example, while growing up, a man saw his father "beaten down by work" (the son's words) and die at an early age of a heart attack. As an adult, he finds he despises work and has a hard time holding a job. In another example, a woman heard her mother say on many occasions, "A marriage is good for about ten years," to explain her many divorces. The daughter finds herself acting out the same pattern in her own life. A man acquired sufficient resources to live comfortably, but feels anxious whenever he spends money. Looking at his past, he recalls his alcoholic father and the financial problems this caused his mother, who was always extremely fearful about not having enough money to feed the family. He still holds this fear.

These are all people trapped in basic assumptions from their pasts that need have no bearing in the present. Until they are recognized and cleared, however, the basic assumptions will keep on operating, coloring every decision and relationship. Using journaling, hypnosis, Vector, or psychotherapy, the Huna student can begin working on identifying and releasing them.

Releasing Harmful Patterns

When thoughts and feelings coalesce around a negative idea, and basic assumptions cluster together, harmful patterns may be created. Some harmful patterns are created by individuals themselves, and others are implanted by those they came in contact with during the course of their lives. The goal of Huna practice is to eliminate harmful patterns and implant your own suggestions so that you aren't being constantly influenced by the patterns of others. Once this has been done, when you do hear an unwanted suggestion, you can be aware of it and cancel it out immediately.

Unwanted behavior that relates to harmful patterns at the Basic Self level includes lying, exaggeration, sarcasm, contradiction, bad manners, cheating, stealing, swearing, selfishness, jealousy, egotism, poverty, wastefulness, greed, allergies, and fears. Lack of anything is related to a harmful pattern, as is an excess of anything. Drugs, alcohol, and smoking frequently involve harmful patterns.

Clusters of ideas that form harmful patterns use up energy and are, in energy terms, alive. Having a lot of negative patterns can cause you to feel tired and depleted. If they aren't erased, they will continue to grow in size. When erasing a harmful pattern, you must eliminate it in the same way it was created—by suggestion to the Basic Self—and replace the negative idea with a correspondingly positive one. When too much negativity accumulates in the Basic Self, it will unload the negativity by means of "accidents" (mishaps) or other physical manifestations such as illness.

For example, one young woman was constantly involved in "accidents." Her automobile was a mass of dents and scrapes where she had been sideswiped and rear-ended. She had been hit by a bus while crossing the street and fortunately escaped with only minor injuries. She broke her arm while playing volleyball and was often cutting or bruising herself. On the face of it, these occurrences were not her fault, and, except for the volleyball accident, involved the participation of others. But why were they happening? Looking at the young woman's history, she had lost her loving parents at an early age and was neglected by an indifferent foster mother. She grew up feeling alone, unloved, and worthless. By the time she reached young adulthood, the woman was carrying around in her Basic Self a heavy burden of grief at the loss of her parents, rage at her foster mother, and feelings of helplessness, victimhood, and lack of self-worth. These patterns manifested in the outside world as things that hurt and damaged her, mirroring the ways in which she felt hurt and damaged as a child. With so much negativity in the Basic Self, she had become "accident-prone." (In the Huna belief system, there are no true accidents.) Eventually, during a particularly low period in her life, this young woman's lack of self-worth became so debilitating that she contemplated suicide and sought help. With love, she began healing her damaged Basic Self. As her mind healed, the accidents ceased.

Releasing Commandments

The Bible's Ten Commandments have been instilled from childhood through religion, family, the society, or all three. While the Commandments may seem like positive rules to live by, remember that the Basic Self takes everything literally. It is confusing to the Basic Self to be told to follow rules that it ends up violating frequently. When it has been instilled into the Basic Self that breaking these rules is committing a sin, then guilt can accumulate every time the rules are broken. But, again, aren't these good rules? In what ways do they lead to guilt feelings in the Basic Self?

Take one example, the injunction against killing, and remember that the Basic Self takes everything literally. Therefore, when your Basic Self hears "thou shalt not kill," it assumes the

Commandment means just that: kill nothing, or do not kill at all. But, consider, normal nonviolent people kill often—they kill weeds, insects, germs, and rodents. If they are hunters, they may go out and kill animals, and if meat eaters, they are condoning the killing of animals by others. To be even more literal, if they are vegetarians, they kill plants. Perhaps they are, or were, soldiers who were directed to kill the enemy. Perhaps they even killed someone else in self-defense. Add to this the murders—both real and fictionalized—seen daily on the news, on television programs, and in the movies, along with the murder mysteries of fiction. These are not "killing" per se, but they do send a signal to the Basic Self that killing is an everyday event.

Indeed, we are surrounded by killing. If the Basic Self has been told that killing is wrong, it naturally assumes that means *all killing*. Therefore, when you kill a spider, pull a weed, cut down a Christmas tree, or watch people being gunned down in a movie, your Basic Self may react with a feeling of guilt and shame. Of course, there are varying degrees of guilt—killing an insect does not engender the same guilt that killing a human would—yet guilt does still accumulate in the Basic Self from this "condoned killing." When framed in a religious context, the action registers in the Basic Self as a sin.

The other Commandments can be just as confusing to the Basic Self. Consider the injunction against adultery. Does the Basic Self know the difference between simply admiring a beautiful woman and "coveting thy neighbor's wife?" or between lusting in your heart and actually committing an act of adultery? What about the Commandment against "coveting thy neighbor's goods"? Does your Basic Self remember it when you admire a new car your neighbor just bought? The Commandment to "remember the Sabbath and keep it holy" might set up a conflict in the Basic Self when you watch a football game on television on a Sunday afternoon or go to a Sunday matinee. Many people say "My God" as an expression. This could be understood by the Basic Self as "taking the name of the Lord in vain."

These seemingly innocent violations of the Ten Commandments may seem trivial and harmless, yet they can actually set up feelings of conflict and guilt at the Basic Self level. Remember also that for the Basic Self, thoughts are things, and the Basic Self can't always distinguish between thought and deed. No actual action need occur—the thought alone is enough to create guilt.

For students of Huna, then, it is helpful to reevaluate the Ten Commandments. Consider how they might be misinterpreted by your Basic Self. Huna students can replace them with only one law: harm nothing with hatred. In Huna, it is intention that is important. Hatred is a powerful emotion, and ill will has the same negative consequences for the self. When you resolve to harm nothing and no one with hatred, you agree to be conscious of your motives. This applies as much to the spoken word as to anything else. Words can hurt, and anything said with malice is harming another. Awareness is the key. The concept of harming nothing with hatred, of course, applies to yourself, and for some, this is the most difficult aspect of the law. Criticizing, being unkind, hurting, and hating others as well as yourself is against the law of Huna.

When it comes to killing, consider all the ways in which you kill in daily life. Resolve never to kill anything, not even an ant, without full consciousness of your actions. Recognize the killing that has gone into providing your daily needs: the trees that were killed to make your paper, the animals that died for your dinner, your jacket, and your shoes. Raise your consciousness to include the welfare of all beings, then resolve to harm nothing with hatred. If you choose to eat animals, do it with consciousness and awareness. Bless the animal you consume and offer thanks to it for giving you life.

Releasing yourself from the literal meaning of the Ten Commandments one by one can free your Basic Self from a load of guilt and shame. The simple commandment to harm no one and nothing with hatred covers a lot of ground. If you follow this, you will not harm others, or your parents, or your spouse, or your neighbor, or strangers, or God. When you do not harm anyone or anything, you also do not bear false witness or steal.

Be assured, when you release the Commandments, you will not become a person without morals or scruples. On the contrary, as you align your Basic Self's truth and your actions in the world, you will become more moral than ever before. You will not be infringing on beliefs held in the Basic Self but will be acting in accordance with higher law. Your Basic Self takes rules far more seriously when they are realistic.

Releasing Sin

It is important to dislodge from the Basic Self belief in sins and the guilt over sins committed in the past. The belief in sin and the awareness of having committed a sin often linger in the Basic Self from childhood and are surrounded by a heavy charge of emotion instilled by a parent or other authority figure. Whether you were raised in a religious environment or not, the concept of sin still permeates the culture. Who has not heard "The sins of the father are visited on the son," and "The wages of sin are death," pronouncements that many Basic Selves take literally? When you are eliminating blocks, it is crucial to remember what you were told was a sin and to clear this from your Basic Self. Was sex a sin? Was lying a sin? Was not going to church a sin? Explore your own upbringing and recall what you were told. If you can't remember, go into the Silence and ask your Basic Self to tell you. Ask if you ever committed a sin.

When you get the answers, you can begin to release yourself from them. The first step is to understand logically (by the Middle Self) that sins must be released. Then the Middle Self must convince the Basic Self that it is advisable to let go of sin. Go into the Silence, invite the High Self to be present, and deal with one sin at a time. Your ritual might go like this: "Dearest Basic Self, Our intention tonight is to release the sin of sex. You were told in the past that sex was a bad thing. The ones who told you did not have this teaching. Sex is a healthy, normal part of our nature, something to be enjoyed and celebrated. There is no sin in sex. The only law we observe is to never hurt anyone—the law of love. In the presence of the High Self, let all my negativity surrounding sex be erased. I am a being who can fully express sex and love. I walk in the light. I am free. So be it. It is done."

When the Basic Self believes a sin has been committed over and over, a sin complex may form—a cluster of ideas and basic assumptions related to one area of behavior. The feelings of guilt may be deep-seated and profound, and the Basic Self may feel so ashamed that it keeps the sin complex hidden away from view by the Middle Self and High Self. To remove a sin complex that you are able to identify, repeat the ritual until a sense of release is felt. Otherwise, it may be necessary to work with a Vector counselor, hypnotherapist, or psychotherapist to reach the deeply held material.

When many harmful patterns are present, a negative ego body can develop that feeds on the energy of the Basic Self and becomes stronger over time. Examples of those with large negative ego bodies are radical leaders and religious fanatics. Spiritual vanity leads to development of a large negative ego. Dissolving negative ego bodies involves working with the Three Selves to speak and think positively, asking for and receiving forgiveness, erasing harmful patterns, and cultivating an understanding and tolerant attitude towards others. Honest humility goes a long way toward erasing a negative ego body and is a sure pathway to the High Self.

Remember that in Huna, there is no true sin, only "missing the mark," and this consists of hurting others intentionally. Though people often don't think of it that way, one form of hurt is judging others.

Releasing Judgments

Judging others can produce toxins in your own system and in those you judge. Judging does not refer to what goes on in a court of law, but what happens between individuals in everyday life when they condemn one another for their differences. Every person is walking in her or his own reality and acting from an individual mindset of experience. If another person's actions harm you physically or mentally, you have a right to speak out. Otherwise, adopt the approach of understanding. Assume a person's actions have a positive motive rather than a negative one. For example, if someone cuts you off in traffic, assume he/she didn't see you, not that it was intentional.

When you form the habit of being nonjudgmental and assuming positive motives, you will be surprised to find how many actions you previously thought were negative really did stem from a positive source. Practice seeing the positive motive in yourself for your own actions. If there are persons you are having difficulty with, work hard to understand them better and see where their motivation comes from. In this way, you will continue to build a positive reality and let others build theirs.

Releasing Criticism

Many people have the problem of being critical towards others. This is actually a form of being critical toward the self. You essentially are seeing faults in others that you don't like in yourself. The result of constantly criticizing yourself and others is to create toxic conditions in your body, your mind, and your world.

Give yourself some time and space to do this ritual and make yourself comfortable. Light a candle and focus your attention. Go into the Silence and take several sets of four slow, deep breaths. Speak (silently or out loud) the following: "Dearest High Self, please assist me in this process, along with my guides, angels, and guardians. Dearest Basic Self, please be fully present and participate in this process. I am here tonight to release the habit of criticism. Criticism has no place on my path. Everyone is free, and I am free, and we are all walking our individual paths in the best way we know how. Dear Basic Self and High Self, guides, angels, guardians, please assist me in releasing forever the habit of criticism. Take all my critical thoughts and transmute them into pure golden light. I now release critical thoughts, critical speech, critical habits. They are all gone from me. I am free. So be it. It is done."

Stay in the Silence and take four more slow, deep breaths. Visualize yourself surrounded by golden light in harmony with all beings in the universe. Come out of the Silence and thank your Selves and all of your helpers.

Releasing Victimhood

One of the surest ways to slow personal growth and to create negativity around you is to feel like a victim. Happily, it is also one of the easiest things to change. People who have been immersed in victimhood for years can free themselves from this state with a simple shift in attitude. The first step is to understand that a prolonged feeling of victimhood has never helped a single person to be better. Feelings of victimization immobilize you. They stop you from taking any positive action because the Basic Self is so involved with feeling injured. Once the Basic Self is freed from this crippling emotional state, you can move forward to make changes in your life. Remember that victimhood only hurts you and never affects what hurt you. With victim thinking and feeling comes powerlessness. Victimhood is toxic to the mind and body.

No matter how devastating something or someone has been to you personally, resolve to end your victim relationship with it or with them immediately. See yourself as a participant in a chain of events. Imagine the events happening again and how you could play a role in them without feeling like a victim. Visualize yourself in a position of strength instead of weakness. Know that the world accepts you according to your own view of yourself. Walk forward from a position of power and think of what action you can take in the future rather than remaining mired in the past.

When you first move away from victimhood, it may be necessary to remind your Basic Self from time to time that you are no victim. Make a habit of changing this thought pattern whenever you feel it coming on. Never think, speak, or let another speak of you as a victim.

Thinking about Money

Money has just as many conflicted attitudes surrounding it as sex and is a stumbling block for many. People grow up with all sorts of opposing and negative assumptions at the Basic Self level regarding money. It is "the root of all evil," it "isn't everything," or "it all comes down to money." "Money," in fact, is symbolic of everything material, and your attitudes toward it reflect your Basic Self's beliefs. Many Basic Selves feel they don't deserve to have money, and a general lack of money can indicate poor self-esteem. Excessive seeking after money can point to a lack of love in the Basic Self. Holding and grasping money shows a deep insecurity. Sometimes the Basic Self has been taught that having or wanting money is sinful and wrong. Many spiritual and religious people have been taught to believe that money is detrimental to living a spiritual life.

Huna, however, emphasizes balance between the spiritual and material realms and advocates a life where both are strong, with one not elevated over the other. Either hating or loving material things throws the self off center. Being strong spiritually and combining this with a healthy material base leads to balance between the Selves, since the Basic Self responds to material things and the High Self exists in the realm of spirit.

Begin to identify your attitudes about money by journaling and requesting information in the Silence. If you encounter negative beliefs or basic assumptions, examine them. Symptoms of negative beliefs are: not having enough money or never feeling that you have enough; fears about not having money in the future; a belief that getting money is a struggle; negative and judgmental feelings toward wealthy people or poor people; hating money; loving money; believing that money can solve all your problems; stinginess; a victim mentality; and excessive shopping and spending. Any of these behaviors indicates that you are out of balance about money.

The first step is to get rid of the notion that money and material things are bad. For those who were conditioned in childhood to believe that money is sinful—the root of all evil—a dialogue in the Silence might go like this: Greet and welcome your Basic and High Selves. "My dearest Basic Self, you may have heard or been told in the past that money is sinful and bad. You may have been told that the love of money is evil. Those who said these things did not have this teaching. Money is not sinful, not bad, not evil. Money is simply a medium of exchange. We are the walking presence of God, and God is rich. Money is green mana, and we have the power to create it and use it whenever we desire. We deserve a rich abundance and a positive material existence. We now release all negative attitudes about money and replace them with positive ones toward money and abundance. We are balanced and happy and we walk in the light. So be it. It is done."

Whatever difficulty you may be experiencing about money, track it back to an assumption held in the Basic Self and set about dispelling it. You can create your own ritual in which you replace whatever it is with a positive assumption about money and material things. Spend some time thinking about what your monetary needs truly are. Imagine yourself already having what you want and see how that feels. Be sure you are ready for what you desire. Then, turn your plan over to the High Self to manifest your goals.

Releasing Fear

For most people, fear is the biggest block of all, and it can manifest as a generalized anxiety or as hundreds of daily fears. Fear has several components; one is false perception. A Huna student once asked Serge King for advice. She had read in the newspaper about a mugging at her automatic teller machine and was now afraid to go there. She asked how to deal with her fears. He replied that if she were to consider this one incident (the mugging) as a basis for her future behavior, she should also consider the thousands of times people had visited the automatic teller machine at that location and not been mugged. To base her behavior on one unusual incident was not logical.

Another reason for fear is not trusting the self. When you love and respect yourself and your abilities, you feel prepared for anything that might come to you. Feeling inadequate leads to fears that you won't be equal to your own life experiences. Cultivate a feeling of confidence in yourself and your ability to deal with anything that might happen. Extend this trust to all the people around you. Expect the best of those around you. When you are able to love and trust all beings, you will project that love, and it will be returned to you.

Many fears do stem from past experience. Just as an animal always remembers a hurt, the Basic Self retains the memories of both emotional and physical injuries. If the hurt represents a pattern, for example, a parent that was habitually hurtful, then the fear may become a complex and lodge deep in the Basic Self.

Learning the source of deep-seated fears is the first step toward releasing them. One student had a fear of being attacked in her home and went to great lengths to secure her doors. She sometimes had dreams of someone breaking into her home.

112

Working with a hypnotherapist, she was able to recall a time in her childhood when an uncle had come to her home when no one else was there and kissed and fondled her. He told her never to tell anyone, and of course, she hadn't. Though the incident had been long forgotten by her, it had created a fear in her Basic Self of not being safe where she lived. This fear had extended to her home, her place of work, and her car. Once she understood the origin of the fear, she released it from her Basic Self.

Generalized fear presents a special challenge. Another student of Huna felt a generalized anxiety but couldn't understand its source, since he had had a happy childhood and could remember no traumatic incidences. Journaling and dialoguing with his Basic Self, he began to understand that his fear stemmed from a period in his childhood when his father went overseas to fight in the war and he was left at home with his mother. His mother was naturally very anxious during the two years her husband was away, though she had tried not to show it to her child. Nevertheless, the mother's Basic Self had communicated the fear to her son's Basic Self, where it remained with him as a kind of free-floating anxiety well into adulthood. No doubt, the fact that the country was at war and that people all around the child had plenty of fear of their own contributed greatly to this generalized sense of menace. Once he discovered the cause of the generalized fear, he was able to erase it from the Basic Self.

HOʻOPONOPONO

The traditional Hawaiian practice called hoʻoponopono literally means "to put to rights," and refers to a family conference in which relationships were set right through prayer, discussion, confession, repentance, mutual restitution, and forgiveness.[12] This valuable therapeutic tool is an ancient practice that remained in the Hawaiian cultural background after Christianity arrived and continued to be used in traditional families. It is receiving a lot of attention these days as families and communities look for a means of resolving problems. It has been called by a modern-day psychiatrist, "one of the soundest methods to restore and maintain good family relationships that any society has ever devised."[13] An excellent source book for further study of hoʻoponopono is E. Victoria Shook's *Hoʻoponopono,* published in 1985, which includes case studies.

The ancient Hawaiians believed that illness and misfortune came from an imbalance in the relationships between people and between people and their gods. They believed that everything in life was related, and thus a problem between two family members was a problem for the whole group. The "family," in a Hawaiian context, included the extended family of relations, adopted children, and close friends.

A hoʻoponopono session was often called when a family member became seriously ill. To the Hawaiian kahuna working to heal a person, a negative entanglement of emotion could block the channel to the gods and made any work attempted with the patient ineffective. The session laid the groundwork for the kahuna healer by revealing the source of the problem. Hoʻoponopono was sometimes used before childbirth in a troubled family, because it was thought that family discord was an obstacle that would hinder the baby's healthy birth.[14] Ho'oponopono could also be called when a family member was made anxious over a bad omen or an ominous dream.

To begin the process of ho'oponopono the family was called together. Family members were expected to make every effort to attend the session and to travel long distances if necessary. Once the family was assembled, the process could take a few hours or it might last for days or even weeks, with multiple sessions.

Ho'oponopono was usually directed by a senior family member, or if the adults were too involved in the situation to be objective, by a family friend or a kahuna known by the family. The session began with a prayer addressed to the family's special guardians, asking that they be present and assist in the process. The rest of the ho'oponopono process followed in a ritualized form that included definite steps. The steps are: identifying the problem, stating the transgression, discussion, identifying the negative entanglement, sharing of feelings, confession, releasing the problem, cutting off the problem, summary and reaffirmation of bonds, and closing prayer.[15]

There were certain rules that were observed when going through these steps. Because the proceedings might be emotional, family members were encouraged to communicate through the leader and to avoid raising their voices and venting angry feelings. Everyone was expected to make a sincere effort to reach the truth in a spirit of openness without hurting or insulting one another. If tempers flared during the session, the leader could call for a cooling off period before continuing.

Family members attempted to get to the root of the problem in a process similar to "peeling an onion." Discussion of the problem invariably would lead to deeper and deeper layers of conflict. Once the problem was identified and discussed at length, the family found ways for its negative aspects to be released. This might involve a person making a confession as well as restitution. Any form of material restitution would be decided and agreed to by all the parties involved. Then, the problem was ritually released *(kala)* and "cut off" *(oki)* by everyone taking part. The leader would summarize what had occurred during the session and make sure all aspects of the problem had been dealt with. There was a reaffirmation of family ties and a closing prayer. The ho'oponopono session usually concluded with a meal.

The second step of the ho'oponopono process—identifying the problem *(kukulu kumuhana)*—has in Hawaiian the expanded meaning of "pooling of strengths, emotional, psychological and spiritual, for a shared purpose."[16] This was the key to the entire process—a mutual coming together on all levels to set things right. In a family setting, this was powerful medicine.

In a modern setting, ho'oponopono can be used by the family and also in groups other than the family, such as businesses, circles of friends, couples, and individuals. Imagine the success of businesses that would hold open and honest sessions among employees when a problem arises. Ho'oponopono can be used effectively between two people without a leader if certain rules are observed. This is described in the "Huna for Everyday" section of this book.

Ho'oponopono is also used by the individual as a part of Huna practice to clear out negativity and blocks so that prayer can be effective, and mana can flow to the High Self. In *Clearing Your Lifepath,* Allan P. Lewis offers a general ho'oponopono to free the mind. It begins: "Infinite Divine Creator, If I, my relatives, or ancestors did ever offend You or Your children by thought, word, or deed, from the beginning of Creation to the present, we sincerely ask forgiveness of You and all concerned. Forgive all our errors and offenses. Forgive all our guilts and resentments. Forgive all blocks and attachments we ever created."[17]

Morrnah N. Simeona, a native Hawaiian who gave workshops in ho'oponopono to groups nationally and internationally, used a written method. She had students write down everything they wanted to clear away in their lives, then it was ritually "kala'd" or released.

An individual ho'oponopono requires a great deal of mental preparation for it to be effective. Spend time with a journal writing your thoughts and feelings about the problem you are having. Be very honest with yourself. Go into the Silence and ask both the High Self and Basic Self for information about the problem. In other words, do the steps of ho'oponopono on your own, identifying, learning about, and fully fathoming your conflict. If you don't do this very important homework, and simply release the problem with a ritual, it may vanish for a time but will come right back. Going to the root of the conflict may involve seeking outside help from a friend, counselor, or health professional. Do what you have to do to explore this area of disharmony in your life. Once you have gone into it fully, find a way to take action on the physical plane to solve the problem. Decide on certain steps to follow in the future and write these down. Make sure both your High and Basic Selves are in agreement with your course of action. Once these have been set down on paper, do the kala or clearing in which you ritually release the problem.

To sum up, ho'oponopono is an immensely useful ritual that can be used in the family, individually, and in many situations of conflict. The Hawaiian principles underlying it are:

1. Unresolved hurt, anger, shame, or guilt can result in physical illness or other disharmony.

2. A problem between two family members affects the entire group.

3. Superficial conflicts are often symptomatic of hidden hurts.

4. Higher powers will assist those who work to resolve their difficulties.

5. There is strength in the shared purpose of a family working together to solve problems.

6. Sincere forgiveness can release negative emotional entanglement.

7. Prayer is essential.

8. Relationships can be healed.

GATHERING MANA

Once the Basic Self is unburdened of negativity and blocks, it can begin to gather an abundant charge of mana. Mana is the basic substance of Huna—its water of life—and without it there is no power to drive the wheel. Mana is gathered every day by the Basic Self—otherwise, the body could not function—and this energy is shared with the Middle Self to fuel the engines of thought. Any surplus mana is used by the High Self to bring your desires into physical form. When mana is low, prayers have little effect. There is literally no energy to manifest your prayers.

How is mana gathered? One of the best ways is known in many disciplines—conscious breathing. The ancient Hawaiians believed that prayer without breath was meaningless, because the prayer had no means of manifesting. Slow, directed, conscious breathing is basic to Huna. Breaths are done in sets of four, a sacred number to the Hawaiians.

You have learned how to go into the Silence and to dialogue with the Basic and High Selves. Go into the Silence (sitting in a chair with your feet on the floor and hands clasped in front of you) and take a series of four slow, deep breaths, holding each one for the count of four and exhaling very slowly through pursed lips. Your breathing should be done without strain or forcing, and there should be plenty of oxygen available in the room (preferably an open window if you are indoors). Repeat this sequence in groups of four until the desired amount of mana is accumulated. This timing is intuitive. You may feel a tingling in your hands when the mana begins to flow into them, and this intensifies as the mana builds up. Continue this process until the flow of mana is palpable. Then, when you feel you have acquired a strong accumulation of mana, separate your hands and open your palms, holding them upward. With your Middle Self, *will* the mana to go to the High Self.

Self-suggestion and visualization are very helpful in this process. The Middle Self asks the Basic Self to create a charge of mana that will be directed toward a specific goal. The Middle Self states the goal and pictures it as if it were already accomplished. The Middle Self visualizes mana rising up to the High Self.

Another method for gathering mana is the following: Sit up straight in a chair, go into the Silence, and take several series of four slow, deep breaths as above. Hold the hands in a cupped position (as though holding a bowl) in front of you about six inches from the body, with fingers firm and facing inward but not touching. Rotate the hands rapidly in a circular motion, one after the other, not touching, six to eight times. Then, pull the hands apart like an accordion while inhaling and bring them together without touching the fingers while exhaling. Repeat the rotating motion four times and the accordion motion four times. While doing this say mentally, "I will a charge of mana to come into my hands." Then after you can feel a charge of mana in your hands, open the palms upward and *will* the mana to the High Self. Attune yourself to the process so that you can feel the energy accumulating in your hands. Continue sending the mana to the High Self until you feel the flow is sufficient. To stop the flow of mana, clasp your hands and rub them together.

HOLDING MANA

Certain elements of nature are filled with abundant mana, and you can share it. Trees and vegetation generally have large amounts of mana. If you feel depleted, sit under a tree and ask the tree to share its energy with you. Then ask your Basic Self to absorb the energy from the tree. Be open and receptive. You are not harming the tree in any way. When you feel you have received enough mana, thank the tree. Ti plants (*Cordyline terminalis*), a plant of the lily family that grows abundantly in Hawaii, have tremendous mana, so much so that it is not advisable to have one in your bedroom—it could keep you from sleeping. Pine trees are especially energizing. In fact, most plants and trees have abundant mana, and unless they are stressed by drought or disease, will energize you by their presence.

Walking on the seashore or alongside any body of water is energizing since water holds and imparts mana. That is why so many people instinctively seek the beach or lakeshore when they go on vacation. Rock formations and caves often are places of powerful mana. Be aware, though, that rocky places inhabited by humans in the past may still hold their mana, and it may not be desirable for you.

Understand that your own personal mana is limited and learn to recognize when it is low. When you become attuned to your own energy levels, you will know when you need recharging. Notice when you are reacting with a lot of emotion to things other people say and "letting things get to you." This indicates that you don't have a buffer of mana around your body to deflect the varied energies in the world around you.

When mana is low, be careful not to allow your Middle Self to push your Basic Self beyond its endurance, or illness could result. Recharge your mana with slow, deep breaths, or do the hand rotation mana gathering exercise described above. When you have accumulated a charge of mana in your hands, hold your palms to your ears without touching the ears. Will the mana to energize you.

Another way of accumulating mana is to spend time sitting in the Silence. Find a quiet place to sit either indoors or outdoors, and take several series of four slow, deep breaths. Then, with your palms open in your lap, focus your mind and then clear it. Visualize in your mind a clear light infused with a color of your choosing and sit in the Silence, breathing slowly and quietly, for ten minutes, letting your mind rest. When thoughts come, gently dismiss them. At the end of the session, clasp your hands together. This is very refreshing and rebuilds mana when it is depleted or when you want to accumulate a charge of mana for healing or other Huna work.

Instead of a color, you can also visualize a peaceful environment, such as a luxuriant Hawaiian garden, a wide seashore, a pine forest, or any other setting meaningful to your Basic Self.

CRAFTING A HUNA PRAYER

When you are ready to begin praying in the Huna way, it is necessary to craft your prayer-request with the utmost care. You want the words to reach the Basic Self in the most effective way. Spend time thinking about what you really do want to come into your life and write it down.

What to Pray For

At this point, students may be asking the question: What do I pray for? Is Huna about getting a new car? About affording a nice house? Having a better love relationship? For healing? Getting a promotion? Developing a rich spiritual life? What do I pray for?

Remember that Huna emphasizes balance. Huna prayer is effective in many aspects of life, and once you learn how to gather mana and direct a prayer, you can put this to work for you in any area. Knowing what to pray for, however, is a product of wisdom that may take many years to grasp and that ultimately has to do with who and what you are. You know by now that it is against Huna ethics to pray for anything that might affect another person, either directly or indirectly. You know also the cardinal rule that Huna practitioners never hurt any form of life with intent or hatred. Combine these two with the concept of balance in all things, and you have the basic guideline for Huna prayer.

People naturally want things to manifest in their lives—new jobs, relationships, soul mates, houses, opportunities for their children. As long as you follow the basic guideline of hurting no one or nothing, of non-interference, and of always working for the highest good, and you keep the High Self involved, you can pray for virtually anything. Let your higher wisdom—your High Self—determine what to ask for and how it will manifest. Be aware when you pray that you are likely to receive what you ask for. You can pray for anything, but it must be suitable for you, and you must be able to handle it for it to do you any good.

Create two sets of goals for yourself: immediate and long-range. Ask yourself what you want to come into your life now and where you would like to be five years and ten years from today. Spend a great deal of time thinking about your goals, weeks if necessary. Write your goals down. Begin visualizing them and setting prayers in motion. Material goals require mana to be gathered; personal spiritual goals simply need to be expressed.

The best prayer-requests are very simple and straightforward. You can ask for "optimum health for the body," "a life of great abundance," "a loving companion," "a harmonious relationship," "confidence in myself," or "spiritual insight." Emphasize the positive aspect of your request.

The more you can visualize what you want, the better, though when it comes to wanting people to come into your life, do not be specific. Picture yourself already having whatever you want to come into your life, and if it's a companion, lover, or friend, visualize yourself walking hand in hand with a person without specific physical attributes. If you are tempted to visualize yourself with someone you know and are attracted to, remember your Huna vow never to influence another person. It is one thing to wish to have a relationship with a specific person, and another to use Huna methods to make it happen. Remember that everyone has free will and that a relationship formed against one person's will is not really in either of your best interests.

Once you have visualized yourself as already having something, hold it in your mind, and do not change it. Feel that you already have it in your life. Do not question how or where it will come to you, and never doubt that you will have it.

Once you have made prayer-requests for yourself, extend your prayers beyond you to your neighborhood, your town, your continent, and your world. Pray for the highest good of all of these.

In praying for healing for others, ask their permission, if possible. If you are unable to ask permission in person, send mana to the High Self in their name and ask that the highest good be done. If you do have permission to help in the healing process, send mana to your own High Self and ask that the mana be shared with the person's High Self to effect healing. Pray regularly and send an abundance of mana. Never visualize disease or disability and ask that it be healed. Always visualize the body or body part as healthy and normal and picture the person healed and happy.

Though kahuna in old Hawaii did do chants and rituals to affect the weather, this is not advisable in our day and time. Our world is too interdependent, and a change in one place might cause problems in another. Also, there are natural patterns beyond the understanding of individual minds and their agendas, and it is not wise to interfere with these. In times of stressful weather, when storms, floods, fires, or earthquakes threaten, pray to the Po'e Aumakua—the Great Company of High Selves—and ask that the highest good be done for the area affected. Better still, ask that the entire planet's weather and geology be balanced for the highest good of the earth and the beings who live here.

The Ha Rite

The word "ha" means "breath" in Hawaiian, and also is the word for the number four. Both breath and the number four had sacred significance for the Hawaiians. Breath is key to raising mana and energizing prayer-actions. The Ha Rite, utilizing both breath and the number four, is a ritualized form of Huna prayer. It requires that you have done your Huna homework, for it will not be effective if blocks exist. By now, you will have learned some methods of freeing yourself of these blocks, and this is extremely important groundwork for this ritual.

Step one is to decide what you wish to pray for. Choose something that is very important to you, and make sure your request is a clear one, you are not infringing on another's free will, and you are sure you can handle the result once the prayer-request is granted. It helps to write down the prayer-request in one succinct sentence so that you have it clarified in your own mind. When you do the Ha Rite, do it for one request at a time—it is more effective if it is very direct and simple. Make sure your terminology is positive and "high-minded" (compatible with the High Self). Instead of wording a prayer to express a lack, word it to express an abundance of health, wealth, or wisdom. Visualize yourself as having this already.

Step two is to provide the setting for the Ha Rite and this can be a place by your altar, or any quiet place that is conducive to the Silence. Bring as much ritual to the Ha Rite as you wish— you may want to place fresh tree branches or flowers on your altar. Candles and incense are wonderful aids to your ritual, as are beautiful gemstones of your choosing that you place on your altar. Hawaiian music or other music that induces an altered state can be played before the ritual to set the mood. Wear loose, comfortable clothing and do the ritual at least two hours after having a meal (in other words, don't do it too soon after eating). The evening hours are the best time to conduct the Ha Rite.

Begin by placing the written prayer-request in front of you on the altar. Go into the Silence, in which you are in a very receptive altered state (though not too deep). With hands clasped in front of you take four sets of four mana breaths in which you breathe slowly and deeply, inhaling on the count of four, holding the breath for the count of four, and exhaling very slowly through pursed lips. Ask your High Self to be present, along with your guides, angels, and guardians. Ask your Basic Self to be fully present and to gather mana for the purpose of the Ha Rite. Visualize the mana welling up in your body like water in a fountain. If you feel you need more mana, continue breathing in sets of four until you feel you have generated a high charge of mana.

When you feel yourself thoroughly charged with mana, state your prayer-request verbally. With your mind, will the mana to be sent from your Basic Self to your High Self for the purpose of granting your prayer-request. Visualize it rising upward. Hold your hands palm up in your lap. Repeat the prayer three more times, four in all, and feel and visualize the mana flowing. Visualize the prayer-request as having already been granted. When you feel enough mana has been sent, close your hands, and then clasp and rub them together to stop the flow.

Say, "The prayer is flown. So be it. It is done." Thank your High and Basic Selves.

The Ha Rite can be repeated for the same prayer-request on succeeding nights or at intervals of a few days. Be very consistent and do not change the wording of your prayer-request in succeeding rites. If possible, do the Ha Rite in exactly the same way each time. If you have different prayer-requests, do them completely separately (it is better to start a new sequence and not overlap). After performing the Ha Rite, it is better not to discuss your prayer-request with others, since they may express opinions or doubts that will affect your Basic Self in a negative way. Think of your Ha Rite as planting a seed and watering it with mana. If your prayer-request is planted in good soil (with blocks removed) and watered with a strong charge of mana, it will bear fruit.

Effective Prayer

Huna prayers can fail for various reasons—one is that a higher purpose may be operating. For example, if you have prayed rightly to the High Self for a result and asked that it be for the greatest good of all, your prayer still may not manifest. Perhaps the desired result was not the best for you or for someone else and was blocked by your High Self. The reason generally becomes clear at a later time. Changing or obtaining a job is a frequent prayer-request, and several true examples are offered here.

A woman living in California decided that she wanted to work in a particular company, doing work for which she was well qualified. Using all the Huna knowledge at her disposal, she made a Huna prayer-action. She did not wish to influence other persons or take another's job, so stated in her prayer that if it were in accordance with her highest good as well as everyone else's highest good, she would like a job to manifest in the company. She gave her prayer-request an abundance of mana. After a number of Huna prayers over a period of several weeks, she began to wonder why nothing was manifesting. She examined her motives, her intention, her prayer-action, and her mana, and found nothing lacking. Assuming that the prayer-action was not in the highest good, she decided to let the matter rest. The following week, the area was struck by a large earthquake, and the company's building was heavily damaged. The building was condemned, and the staff had to move to temporary quarters in most uncomfortable circumstances. That the woman's prayer included the request that it be for everyone's highest good was fortunate, since getting the job prior to the earthquake would not have been a desirable outcome for her.

Another reason for failure might be that the Basic Self has some issues surrounding the realization of the prayer and blocks it. When a prayer fails to get results, question both the Basic Self and the High Self in the Silence to find out the reasons. Prayers may be answered in time, but may manifest very slowly if not enough mana has been created. If your prayer manifests but has some negativity attached to it, it reflects negative thinking on your part. For example, a man left his job because he intensely disliked his employer. He made a Huna prayer-action asking that a lucrative job manifest for him. The job manifested quickly—he was soon offered a good job at a good rate of pay—but soon found that he did not like his new supervisor either. He then did some soul searching and in taking an honest look at his work history, he realized that he had worked for many "bad bosses," and usually ended up leaving because of them. He had seen this as coincidence but in looking at the pattern, he realized he had a problem. In delving into it further, he discovered he had a mindset of resentment against "working for someone else" lodged in his Basic Self. He set about changing this basic assumption, and using a Huna ritual, he was able to dispel the resentment he felt toward employers in general. That left him free to find another job that included both good pay and a good boss, which he did.

Sometimes when you pray "for everyone's highest good," you open yourself to unexpected circumstances. A particularly gifted elementary school teacher who was new to Huna felt burnt out by his job and wanted to move on to something else. He began looking for a new job outside teaching and did a Huna prayer-action asking that a good opportunity manifest for him elsewhere. He included in the request that everything happen "for the highest good of all." After several months, his job search had produced no results, and he became discouraged. He then consulted an experienced Huna practitioner to help him understand the failure of his prayer. The Huna practitioner went into the Silence and asked her High Self why the prayer had not manifested. The answer surprised them both, since it had nothing to do with blocks in the teacher's prayer-request (as he had suspected). It seems there was a little boy in the teacher's class who was having family problems and desperately needed a role model and authority figure at that time. The teacher had been paying attention to him and taking special care with him, and this was making a big difference in the child's life. It was not in the highest good of this boy that his teacher leave him at that time. The outcome of the situation was that the teacher awakened to the realization that he really was making a difference with his students and decided to stay on in teaching. Ultimately, the outcome proved to be for his highest good, too.

CUTTING THE AKA CORDS

Aka cords consist of energy patterns that you establish with anything you touch, feel, or think about. They can be visualized as light, elastic, stringlike connections between you and people, places, or things. As your association with the people, places, or things continues and grows, these slender cords strengthen until they can appear as thick as ropes or chains to the sensitive person who can intuit them. Aka cords are being described when people talk of "tying the knot," "cutting ties," "the ties that bind," "family ties," "hanging loose."

Though aka cords occur naturally, they do not always serve you. You may have ties to places you wish to leave or to persons you wish to part from. Having heavy ties between you and certain others may not be in your best interests. Ties to a parent, a friend, a home, or a possession may actually be a drain on your energy.

It is desirable to cut aka cords between yourself and family, friends, places, and things from time to time. When moving from one house to another, cut the aka cords between you and your former home so that others can make it their own and feel comfortable there. Do the same when you buy a new car. Cut the aka cords to friends, acquaintances, or relatives who no longer enhance your life. When you give things away, such as clothes or books, cut the aka cords you have established with them.

Huna teachers Jack and Josephine Gray led a ritual in their Huna classes in which their students cut all the aka cords they had ever created in their lives. For this ritual, they asked the assistance of Archangel Michael, the special helper of Huna practitioners, to cut the ties with his sword. Archangel Michael, they explained, is a powerful and universal energy being who transcends cultures and traditions. The qualities this highly evolved being brings are action, justice, compassion, and wisdom, all very helpful in cutting through long-established aka cords.

Cutting the aka cords is a liberating experience that leaves you free to move forward into a future of your own choosing. Do not be concerned that you are going to lose valued relationships with people you love. Your energy connections will return the instant you feel love for the person.

Be in a positive, peaceful mood for this ritual. Give yourself space and time. It can be done alone or in a group, and it is quite powerful when people with one intention work together. If you are doing it in a group, stand with several feet of space between you. Lower the lights, and light candles if possible. Begin by closing your eyes and taking several sets of four slow, deep breaths. Ask both your Basic Self and your High Self to be fully present and to assist you. Invite all of your guides, angels, and guardians to be present and assist you. Begin by saying aloud (or in a group, have one person say aloud): "My dear Basic Self and High Self, please be fully present. Dearest guides, angels, and guardians, please assist me (us). It is my intention tonight to cut all the aka cords I have ever formed between myself and other people, other places, and objects from the beginning of time. This will free me completely. I ask Archangel Michael to come and bring his powerful, shimmering sword to assist in this process."

Take several more sets of four slow, deep breaths until you can feel the mana in your hands. Then hold your arms outstretched. Say: "Here, before the Basic Self, High Self, and guides, angels, and guardians, I ask Archangel Michael to attend, bringing his mighty sword. I ask him now to cut all the aka cords that have ever formed between me and others." Keep your arms outstretched.

Picture Archangel Michael descending in a haze of gold and blue light with his dazzling sword. Visualize him cutting through all the energy cords around you and see them dissolve into nothingness. Using your right hand, make symbolic cutting motions around your body. Then stand back and see how it feels to have no aka cords. Feel the new you, reborn, free, clear, and happy. Feel the sense of limitless freedom and immense independence.

Thank Archangel Michael for his help and thank all of your guides, angels, and guardians. Thank your Basic and High Selves. Repeat: "Thank you, universe, for your love and your caring as I walk forward as a new being, free and clear of all ties."

You can do this ritual again after several years or when you feel it is needed. When you wish to cut the aka cords to anyone or anything, you can simply take deep breaths and then use your right hand to cut the ties, stating your intention to sever them.

IF EVERYONE PRACTICED HUNA

Huna is all about the power of the mind to create reality. Now that you have worked with your Three Selves and have learned to manage energy, release blocks, and pray effectively, it is intriguing to ask: what if everybody did?

First of all, if everyone believed that thoughts and words had a great deal to do with creating individual reality, there would be a lot more attention paid to the spoken word. If 80 percent of human speech is negative, think how much behavior would change if speech were 80 percent positive. This would be a real challenge for the news media, television, and the movies.

Consider the implications of the Huna Vow. If everyone resolved to truly take care of their own lives and their business and let others walk their paths in peace, there would be much greater tolerance and less criticism. Negative campaigning would be a thing of the past, and all advertising would have to be very, very honest.

Imagine how society would change if everyone worked to release harmful patterns at the Basic Self level. With sexual impulses freed and channeled into healthy paths and old angers released, there would be little violence among peoples. With forgiveness of self and others throughout all time, there would be no more reason for wars between ancient enemies. If conflicts arose, they could be addressed with ho'oponopono at the highest levels between peoples or nations. Not hurting another would operate as the basic rule of behavior.

If people truly understood their own energy—their mana—they could engage in activities that gathered mana and thus live in an optimal way, feeling good, and avoiding much illness. If illness came, they would see it as a message and begin searching for the life cause while helping the body back to health with remedies on the mental, spiritual, and physical planes.

In a Huna world, prayers would become a way of life and fill the planet with happiness, abundance, and health. Once the individuals' needs were met, they would be free to help others reach their highest and best good.

Meaningful ritual would become a part of life, and people would spend time in nature connecting with their source. Silence and meditation would be valued by all.

If everything in existence were seen as a manifestation of God, with all of nature connected, exploitation of others—races, cultures, and different life forms—as well as misuse of the environment, would cease. Individuals would realize they are not alone and have a High Self to help them through life, as well as loving spiritual guides, guardians, and angelic beings.

In this Huna world, balance would be the ideal, and people would work to restore balance to their relationships and to their environment. Balance between the Three Selves would be valued, with the High Self providing the spiritual guidance, the Middle Self offering logic and reason, and the Basic Self contributing the physical means, feelings, mana, and love. More and more, people would learn to operate at the level of the High Self, seeing the higher purpose of things and bringing their everyday actions to a higher plane.

Life would consist of equal amounts of work, rest, education, and play. Leisurely activities to restore the Basic Self and give rest to the Middle Self would be highly esteemed, and it would be seen as important to make time for them. Arts, music, and dance would be considered essential elements of the joy of life.

Balance between the material and the spiritual worlds would be practiced, so much more time would be spent in spiritual activities. A comfortable materialism for every being would be the goal, but beyond that, accumulating goods would not hold much significance.

Finally, authority figures would not hold the power they do today. The emphasis would be on acting from a place of personal responsibility for the good of all.

Though the world may seem far from all of this right now, just by reading this book you have begun the journey toward making it a reality. Using your powers of visualization, see this Huna world as a reality, and imagine how it would look and feel. Then, with your new Huna knowledge, make this your own world today.

Huna for Everyday

Once you have mastered the basics of Huna concepts and practice, you can extend these to many different areas of life to make things easier for yourself. Max Freedom Long once wrote that if you are not using Huna, you are working too hard. Those words have been proven time and time again.

These practical techniques are listed alphabetically for easy reference. They have been tested by the experience of Huna students and teachers, but as always in Huna, nothing is carved in stone (except petroglyphs). Feel free to make your own rituals using Huna concepts or to modify these, and keep notes on the techniques you use that obtain reliable results. These can be shared with other Huna students in a Huna periodical such as *The Huna Work International*.

ABUNDANCE

Huna teaches harmony between the spiritual and the material worlds, and it can help you manifest abundance in your life. A good money ritual can increase your material wealth, but before performing one, you need to have done the work with the Basic Self to release your negative attitudes toward money. Otherwise, the assumptions held by your Basic Self will negate the effects of the ritual.

Once you have identified your attitudes toward money (which are often very similar to your parents' views), and released any negativity, you are in a position to perform an abundance ritual. If you can, wear the colors green and gold for this exercise, since they hold the vibration of abundance and will make an impression on your Basic Self. Go into the Silence and take a series of four slow, deep breaths, exhaling slowly. Ask your Basic Self to fully participate and ask your High Self to be present to assist you in the ritual. Then, visualize yourself surrounded by a sea of money—gold, checks, cash, and coins—with so much of it that you have plenty for yourself and others. Smile at the sight of so much abundance and the fact that you are in the center of it. Notice any feelings of discomfort you have or feelings of not deserving the money and address these feelings.

Once you are feeling quite comfortable surrounded by money, begin to toss the money into the air in wild abandon, celebrating the sheer beauty and quantity of it. See yourself tossing substantial amounts of money to every being on earth from your inexhaustible supply. See the smiles on the faces of the others as they take their large gifts and go away happy. See everyone on earth having a superabundance of this "green mana." After you have supplied everyone on earth with as much as they will ever need, look down at your feet. You are still knee deep in money of every kind. Smile at its green and gold abundance.

Repeat these words: "My dear Basic Self, we are surrounded by a supply of money that will never run out. We are living in a state of total abundance. Whenever we want to see the colors of green and gold—of green mana—in our lives, we need simply visualize it, and it manifests. It is very easy to do this. All abundance is ours, and we are rich beyond measure. So be it. It is done."

You will find that generosity creates more abundance in your life than any other practice. When you give freely of what you have, you are acknowledging the richness of the universe of which you are a part. Giving away part of your income to help others is magical and will return wealth to you many fold.

Be mindful of believing that money can transform your life. Some people think of money as the answer to every problem, the magic key that will unlock their happiness. "If only I had the money," goes a common refrain, "I wouldn't have to work at this job I hate, I wouldn't have to live in this house, I could buy a new car, I could move away, I could travel around the world, I could make my dreams come true..." This way of thinking emphasizes a perceived lack and only creates more lack (or perception thereof). Begin to adjust your thinking. Begin with figuring out just exactly what it is you want to do in your life, then set about making that happen. Do not let "not having the money" deter you. For example, if you desire money so that you don't have to work, you are probably in the wrong job. Everyone needs a reason to get up in the morning and needs something meaningful to do, no matter how much money they have. Instead of simply wishing for money to free yourself, begin manifesting a new job that you love and work that you want to do. If your problem is poor living conditions or the need for better transportation, begin planning, even in a very modest way, to make a change for the better in those areas. If you desire money to travel, instead of just staying at home and feeling that you can't afford it, figure out a way to travel and get paid for it. You could get a job on a ship or an airline or in some other aspect of the travel industry. In other words, do the abundance ritual and manifest the cash, and also begin working on making your dreams come true. You do not need to wait until you manifest money for your goals. Rather, you can manifest them directly and have money, too.

"ALCHEMY" MEDITATION

Changing anxious thought patterns is like changing your swimming stroke when you're in the middle of the stream—it is difficult to stop being anxious when you already feel that way—but releasing your anxieties is ultimately the only way to make changes in your reality.

When you find yourself beset by fearful thought patterns that produce anxiety, and you have no clue as to how to break out of the worry cycle, there is a meditation you can do that is quite effective. It is based on the certainty that your High Self knows what to do when you don't and is ready and able to help you. In this meditation, you offer up your thoughts, your situation, and your entire life to the High Self and ask it to transform all of these for your highest good.

In the "Alchemy" Meditation, your "baser" thoughts—your anxieties—are transformed by the High Self into the God realm of pure gold. Find a quiet spot and go into the Silence, taking sets of four slow deep mana breaths, inhaling slowly, holding the breath for the count of four, and exhaling slowly with pursed lips. Ask your High Self and your Basic Self to be present. Then take all of the toxic and anxious thoughts at both the Basic and Middle Self levels and offer them up to the High Self. Only you will know what your toxic thoughts are.

You might say, "My dearest High Self, I offer you all the anxious thoughts I have about my parents, about my children, about my mate, about my friends, about my job, about my house, about my car, about my safety, about the future, about my entire life. I offer you all the stressful thoughts I have about myself and all of my fears about not being good enough. Please take all of these feelings completely away from me and transform them by your powerful golden light. I am giving up the thoughts to you now. So be it. It is done."

Visualize your thoughts ascending to the High Self where they are enfolded in beautiful shimmering golden light and transformed into a higher substance. Send the negative thoughts from both the Middle Self and Basic Self levels, since these will be different. For example, the Middle Self might have frustrations with other people's behaviors or with the performance of a task. The Basic Self might have unspecified feelings of fear, anxiety, and inferiority.

After your request, you will feel the tension and anxiety literally leave your body and ascend to the High Self into golden light. You are then likely to feel an emptiness in your body where the feelings and stress resided. Ask the High Self to send you light and color to fill these spaces, then fill them with vibrant hues—emerald greens, lapis blues, clear energizing reds, dancing yellows, ethereal purples, and all the colors of the rainbow, plus glowing white light and pure golden light, as appropriate. These will come into you and fill the empty spaces where your anxieties were. Thank the High Self for taking your thoughts and for replacing them with color and light.

Afterwards, whenever you feel the return of an anxious thought pattern, remind yourself that you gave them all to the High Self and send the stray thought on its way upward.

ALTARS

An altar is a sacred space that focuses the attention and holds the energy of your spiritual purpose. As a center for your spiritual practice and a place where you keep your ritual elements, it is an expression of your connection with the divine. Create a Huna altar that you can use for ritual and meditation. It does not have to be elaborate and may contain any elements that bring you to a contemplative state and remind you of your purpose. For students of Huna, basic altar pieces might be:

- Candles (be mindful of safety and place candles in containers where they will not fall over);

- A candle snuffer (because you lose a small amount of mana when you blow out a flame);

- A bag or container of salt that has been purified and charged with mana; sea salt is preferable, but any kind of salt will do. When sprinkled about the house or altar area, the salt purifies and energizes the space;

- A container of water that has been charged with mana; the water can be from a place that is special to you or a sacred site;

- A ti leaf or a pine branch, and/or flowers;

- Seashells, special stones;

- Images or carvings of the goddesses, gods, angels, or guardians you work with;

- Pendulums, stones, shells, and cards used as oracles. With practice, you can learn to use these accessories to get answers from your High and Basic Selves.

Keep your altar clean and tidy, and use it often. Make it the focus of your Huna practice and it will acquire its own mana. After a while, just being near the altar will raise your vibration and put your Basic Self into a receptive state.

AMULETS AND TALISMANS

An amulet or talisman is something you wear or carry that will assist you in your personal goals, radiate a protective field, and energize you with its mana. All substances have their own properties, but they can be enhanced with mana. You can store mana in objects made of ivory, hardwood, gold, and silver, to name a few. Crystals have their own powerful vibrations and can be enhanced with mana, but you should be careful about wearing them about the body. Since they are powerful, you need to experiment with them and be conscious of the effects they are having on the body.

Precious stones are highly evolved rocks that have their own unique characteristics. When it comes to gemstones, do not depend on what others have said or written about their effects, since these can vary with the individual wearer. Experiment with them and find out what works best for you. When you find a stone or object that resonates with your energy, wear it around your neck. Protective amulets are best worn on the hand so they can work in your outer aura.

Some special amulets that can be used to enhance the practice of Huna are the following:

Amber is an ancient substance composed of the fossilized resin of extinct evergreen trees that lived millions of years ago. Amber can be easily charged with mana and will energize you when worn about the body. Be aware that amber can also hold the vibrations of others, so it is wise to thoroughly strip it of past energy before it is charged. Baltic amber is excellent for this purpose, with the best being the clear reddish golden brown color that has given the color its name. Dominican amber, which tends to be golden or red in color, and other forms of amber are also good. Discoidal fissures and plant debris in the amber give it extra beauty and enhance the energy.

Red coral. The reddish orange coral that has given its name to the color, as well as the redder shades, has a powerful protective energy when worn around the neck or on the hand. It is useful for repelling entities and negative vibrations and is very helpful if worn when you are moving among large crowds of people. Black coral is also protective but in a more passive way than the red. Coral is best worn in its branch form, but can be effective in other forms. Pink coral has a lovely balancing vibration. Be mindful of the source of the coral for reasons of ecology.

Garnets are excellent for Huna practices and can be charged with mana to enhance the stone's own clearing and energizing effects. Look for larger stones with a vibrant ruby/red color.

Ivory has wonderfully protective properties, as well as a calming effect on the body. Be sure to purchase only antique or fossil ivory and be aware, just as with coral and pearls, that this is a substance from living beings. Select and wear these with consciousness.

Pearls have the ability to clarify intentions and connect you with your High Self. They need not be charged with mana, but will radiate their own luminous energy.

Symbols are powerful stimulants to the Basic Self when they are meaningful to the wearer. Choose amulets made of metals and other natural substances that can be charged with mana and worn about the body. Ankhs, petroglyph figures such as the Rainbow Man, and spirals are all good Huna symbols to wear.

To charge your amulets and talismans, do the following ritual in which you imbue the object with mana from the High Self:

1. It is best to do this ritual at night. In a quiet place, go into the Silence and take several sets of four slow, deep breaths. Place the amulet in front of you on an altar or table. Have a paper cup of water nearby. Ask your Basic Self and your High Self to assist you, along with your guides, angels, and guardians.

2. Visualize the amulet in its virgin state. If it is a piece of amber, see it as sap oozing from pine trees in the primeval forest; if it is coral, as part of a living reef; if you are using gemstones, see them as raw beauty hidden deep in the earth. See the object as pure and fresh as it was at the time of its creation.

3. Ask that the object be cleared and cleansed of all vibrations it has acquired since its creation. See it as completely cleansed. Pass your right hand over the object, without touching it, and "pull off" all vibrations it may have acquired, tossing them into the cup of water. Say as you do this: "I am now stripping this object of all vibrations it has acquired from any source from the moment of its creation to the present time." Pass your hand over it several times. Visualize the object as cleared and cleansed.

4. Then hold your hands with palms downward over the object and take several series of four deep mana breaths, asking the High Self to energize the object with mana. You are being a conduit for mana from the High Self. Feel light and energy coming from the High Self and permeating your hands and the object. Feel great love, peace, and harmony entering the object. Sit quietly and let this energy flow from above.

5. Close your hands to stop the flow and thank the Basic Self and High Self. Discard the water down the drain or outside where there is no vegetation, and throw away the paper cup. When you are not wearing the amulet, keep it wrapped in a soft material such as cotton or velvet and tucked away in a small box. The energizing process can be repeated after a period of time.

Always follow your guidance when working with objects. You should notice beneficial effects right away from an amulet that has been charged with mana. If you don't, or if you feel some strange effect from the amulet, ask your Basic Self to give you feedback on it. Perhaps it's not right for you. Be very cautious about wearing jewelry, stones, metal, or other objects that have not been stripped and energized with mana from the High Self. Often, when someone who loves you gives you a gift of jewelry, it will come charged with abundant personal love. This can be a wonderful piece to wear for a time; however, the situation may change if you become estranged from that person. At that point, you have a choice: either return the gift or strip it of its vibrations.

In the case of a piece with a heavy charge, such as a wedding ring, you will have to convince the Basic Self to give up the strong associations it has with the piece as well as stripping it.

You can charge a stone or piece of jewelry to give to another person as long as the mana comes from the High Self. Don't charge watches, since the charge of mana could interfere with their accuracy or cause them to stop working altogether. Let the person know you have charged the piece with spiritual energy. In one incident, a Huna student charged a lovely garnet that was set in a gold pendant with mana during a group session, then gave it to her mother as a gift. She did not think to mention that it had been charged. Two weeks later, her mother asked her what she "had done to the pendant." When the student said it had been charged with mana, her mother replied that she had only asked because whenever she wore it, her sinuses cleared up.

ANIMAL ALLIES

The ancient Hawaiians had a complex relationship and a great deal of interaction with the animal world. Once you begin to feel a connectedness with all of life, you understand that animals, birds, and sea creatures do not exist to serve humans but are their own form of being with their own unique experience of existence. A more helpful approach to living things is to see them as allies on planet earth with their own wisdom to impart.

Consider the animals you encounter in your world and study them closely. See things from their point of view. You will likely feel drawn to certain animals more than others. Erika S.

Nau, the author of *Huna Self-Awareness,* describes the Basic Self's affinity with certain animal characteristics. She finds it helpful for Huna students to discover the animal that most closely relates to their Basic Selves.

Spend time with the animals of your choosing and learn their wisdom. Nurture them and help them and you will receive a great deal in return. Listen to their advice and listen for messages that the Basic Self and the High Self send through them. Communicate with animals through your feelings and through mental pictures.

AURA PURIFICATION

The kahuna used water for purification and blessing and as a symbol of mana. Salt water was used in ritual, and some rituals, such as ho'oponopono, often concluded with an ocean bath. When you have been in crowds or negative situations, purify the body with water. If you don't live by a natural body of water such as the ocean or a lake, take a "mana shower." Standing under the flowing water, ask the mana in the water to energize you and to wash away all negative vibrations from your aura. Feel any negativity you have rolling off of you down the drain. When you take a shower in the morning, ask the High Self to cleanse you of negativity and for the water to take all negativity out to the ocean to be purified.

CHANTS

Chants combine elements that are well-known to the Hawaiians: the spoken word, rhythmic sound, and powerful intention, in a way that dramatically involves all Three Selves. Chants invoked the gods and raised mana while communicating with the universe in a direct way. In David K. Bray's words, "The sounds of the chants act as a bridge between kahuna and Aumakua. There may be no apparent physical change, but during a chant a psychic and spiritual transformation takes place, which may work itself out in material form in many time patterns."[18] Gourds and drums were used to increase and enhance the mana.

If you intend to work with chants in Hawaiian, be advised; Hawaiian chants are not playthings. Do not attempt to reproduce Hawaiian chants unless you are also delving deeply into their meanings and able to understand their intended effects. If you do wish to chant in Hawaiian, work with a teacher who understands the meaning of the words and can coach you. Otherwise, compose your own chants in your own language and with your own sounds.

Kellie Koucky, a Huna teacher in California, uses what she terms "Spirit Chants" to help students progress on their paths. At a Huna Research Seminar workshop, she said, "Sound is transformational. It breaks down old structures in order to create new ones. Chanting with spirit can move energy through the blocks of self-hatred and low self-worth—through blocks so strong they can cause disease conditions. Chanting allows movement of energy that enables healing of the spirit, mind, and body" (Lecture, June 12, 1999). She advocates creating your own chants using free, uninhibited sounds and tones that you respond to—sounds that reflect your own unique vibrational qualities and vital life force. She often has students draw images of their chants with crayon and paper to reproduce the visual dimension of sound.

For further raising your vibration and healing your soul, listen to Hawaiian chants by Aunty Edith Kanaka'ole and other legendary Hawaiians as well as chants from the world's cultures—the African, Native American, European, and Polynesian sounds of the spirit.

COMMUNICATION WITH ALL THINGS

The Hawaiians found conscious connection everywhere. Indeed, the individual is connected with everything since all things are the same energy that vibrate at different rates. This applies to so-called inanimate objects as well as animate ones. You are always in relationship to the things around you. For instance, when you sail on a ship on the ocean, you are in relationship to the vessel you are in, to the winds, to the ocean, and to the creatures in the sky and sea, as well as to the people on board. You also have the potential to be able to communicate with all of these elements. You are an integral part of your environment at all times, and it is a part of you.

It is easier to feel in relationship to nature when you are in a forest or at the seashore, but you are just as much a part of your environment when you are sitting at your desk in your office on the ninth floor. Form the habit of awareness of your environment and be sensitive to your relationship to it, no matter where you are. Be receptive to the elements in your immediate environment and have a dialogue with them. In communicating with other forms of existence, you must be both impersonal and humble and be willing to communicate at their level. An attitude of reverence is important.

CREATIVITY

Creativity flows when the Three Selves are in balance, and mana is abundant. Blocks of any kind in the creative process are literally the same blocks that hinder the flow of mana between the Selves. When all three are in good working order, the Middle Self sets the direction and provides the structure while the High Self provides the inspiration. The Basic Self contributes the physical stamina, the memory, and the input of the senses.

You cannot think your way into creativity. In order to be truly creative, you have to relax the Middle Self's grip so that ideas flow from the High Self. Your means of creative expression must appeal to the Basic Self, or the Basic Self will block the process. Most "writer's block" stems from boredom at the Basic Self level. No matter how fascinating your intellect finds a project, you must engage the Basic Self or the work will be blocked. When inspiration is flowing from the High Self, the Basic Self is participating physically and emotionally, and the Middle Self is providing practical guidance, wondrous things can result.

DEITIES

If your spirit resonates with Hawaii and for many students of Huna, it does, then you may want to interact with Hawaiian deities. When you want a certain quality (associated with a specific deity) to come into your life, go into the Silence and focus your attention on the deity. Ask that the wisdom, strength, creativity, or other quality be transmitted to you directly. Be very respectful and thankful. To strengthen your connection, create an altar with elements from nature that relate to the deity.

Kane is a god who represents higher wisdom and power. Kane is associated with the heavens, the sacredness of life, the elements, fresh water as well as the mystical water of life, thunder, mist, and clouds.

Hina is an ancient goddess closely linked with the moon and lunar wisdom. She is associated with healing herbs, women's work, and fertility. Among her elements are seawater, coral, tapa cloth, and the colors gray or silver.

Ku is a god who embodies the active principle in nature. Ku is the facilitator, the doer, and is associated with the sun. "Ku" means "to stand or rise upright." Ku's energy is action-oriented, forward-looking, logical, and effective.

Laka is the goddess of the hula, the sacred dance of Hawaii. Laka is associated with beauty, joy, grace, sacredness, physical harmony, closeness to nature, and spiritual growth. Her manifestations are the greenery of the deep forest, fragrant flowers, divine dance, and song.

Lono is a god linked with the earth, agriculture, rain, and fecundity.

Pele is the goddess of the volcano, synonymous with the power underlying all creation; a dynamic, loving force for change. Associated with transformation, Pele's energy destroys, yet builds in the process.

Maui is the beloved adventurer-god of Polynesia. Maui is known for his legendary acts such as pushing up the heavens, fishing up islands, and snaring the sun. He is also the trickster who gets into tight situations and extricates himself. He is associated with the qualities of bravery, an adventurous spirit, direct action, a sense of humor, competency, travel, and risk-taking.

Uli is a discerning goddess who sees clearly, and is associated with medicine and healing.

DREAM INTERPRETATION

Hawaiians considered dreams far more important than we do today. They looked upon dreams as messages from the spirit world and took the time to interpret them. Symbols in dreams were significant. The High Self sometimes communicated through dreams and could give advice, warnings, or answers to problems.

Write down any dreams you have that are particularly vivid and that occur immediately before waking. Pay attention to those that take nightmare form and that have a feeling of significance to you. Write or type them out double-spaced. Then, using a good dream book such as Betty Bethards',[19] write the meanings underneath the dream text, noting only the meanings that feel right to you. This should enable you to read the true meaning of the dream. You can also do this using your own meanings. Clear your mind and ask for images that relate to the dream symbols, then write them down.

When you begin to work with dreams, you will find that you will begin to remember them more often. If you are having trouble remembering your dreams, before going to sleep, ask your Basic Self to cooperate with you in bringing your significant dreams to the conscious level.

FINDING LOST OBJECTS

When you can't find your keys or other objects, you can access information directly from your Basic Self. Your Basic Self knows where the lost object is located and will supply it to you if you can create certain conditions. To make this work, you must be able to calm your mind.

It is very frustrating to lose something—whether it is the keys, your eyeglasses, or an important document in your office. The scenario is often as follows: you are ready to leave the house for an appointment and you can't find your car keys. You search everywhere. You realize if you don't leave now you are going to be late. You search the house with increasing frustration. Then you become angry. At this point, you remember Huna (it would go easier if you would recall it before the anger sets in).

Sit down. Clear your mind. Remind yourself that you have it in your power to find your keys, and that your Basic Self knows where they are. Take four slow, deep breaths. Focus your mind and clear it of all thought. Let the anger go. Once you have achieved a calm state of mind, continue to breathe slowly.

Hold your left hand, palm up, in your lap. Then, communicate with your Basic Self as follows. Be sure to underscore the importance of finding the item.

155

"My dear Basic Self: I am in great need of my keys. I need to drive the car to go to this appointment. This appointment is very important to me. Please help me now. Please access your memory and reveal to me the location of the keys."

Sometimes, at this point, an image of the lost object's location will flash into your mind. If this doesn't happen, continue, asking, "Are the keys in this house?" Listen for an internal voice that communicates a yes or no answer quickly. Perhaps you will feel a definite impression of yes or no. If the answer is yes, walk slowly to one room and stand at the threshold. Ask, "Are the keys in this room?" Listen for the answer. If the answer is no, move to the next room. If yes, walk slowly to the center of the room and, with left hand in front of you, palm facing outward, ask your Basic Self to lead you to the keys. Allow your body to turn in any direction that it wishes. Your Basic Self will usually lead you directly to the object.

Using this technique, one Huna student reported that he found a watch that had fallen under the cushions of a sofa. A woman found a ring that had dropped to the bottom of a box of Christmas decorations. Both had no clue where or when their items had been lost. Some Huna students report a tingling in the outstretched left hand when the object is nearby.

If you receive an answer that the object is not in the house, ask for a mental image of its location. Asking your Basic Self for assistance, take several sets of four mana breaths and send the mana to the High Self. Explain to both Selves how important the lost object is to you and state your desire to have it back. Ask that it find its way back to you.

When you retrieve the lost keys or other lost item, thank the Basic Self and praise it for its marvelous memory. Then, reflect on why you lost the item in the first place. Often your Basic Self, the seat of memory, will "go on strike" because of stress or tension related to the item. Perhaps the nature of your destined appointment produced anxiety in the Basic Self. Perhaps you were not feeling well, and the Basic Self really wanted to stay at home. Look for a conflict between your Middle and Basic Selves. Lost items can have symbolic value. If you lose a watch, perhaps your Basic Self is protesting that you live too much "by the clock" with no time for relaxation. If you often lose your car keys, perhaps you are "driving yourself" too hard and too fast.

Some people lose jewelry, wallets, keys, and other items habitually. This is a strong message from the Basic Self to the Middle Self that a problem exists that you are not addressing. This is the Basic Self's way of trying to capture your attention— depriving you of things that both of you value.

Occasionally, you will lose items that your Basic Self has rejected as not good for you. Pieces of jewelry and clothing that do not harmonize with the body may be "lost" by the Basic Self as a form of self-protection. If this is the case, your efforts to access the Basic Self's memory may not work. One student lost his glasses and used all the Huna methods he knew to retrieve them, but nothing worked. Though it wasn't time for an eye exam, he decided to have one anyway. It turned out that his eyes had improved and he needed a new prescription.

If you want to assist other persons in finding items they have lost (when your Basic Self was not present), you can contact your High Self for assistance. In the Silence, ask for information to be transmitted through the network of the Great Company of High Selves to you. Another way of assisting others is to use the pendulum to dowse the location of the lost item.

FLOWERS AND PLANTS

Flowers and plants figure prominently in Hawaii's cultural lore for their curative and restorative powers and their connections to the gods. All cultures value them for their contribution to the pure joy of living. Two sacred flowers to the Hawaiians were the *ilima,* a lovely, delicate yellow/orange flower treasured for leis—garlands—and the red *lehua* blossom, sacred to Pele, Laka, and Hina. Fragrant *maile,* a vine that grows in the mountains, is sacred to Laka and used as an offering. It is made into leis for sacred or ceremonial occasions. The nuts from the *kukui* tree had many practical uses in old Hawaii, and today are used for sacred or ceremonial leis. Kukui nuts are filled with oil and can hold a strong charge of mana. The *awa* plant was considered sacred for the analgesic properties of its root and was often used in ritual. *Olena* or turmeric had many practical uses and was used by the kahuna in purification rituals.

The green ti plant (pronounced like "tea") was used by the ancient Hawaiians for practical purposes—food was often served on ti leaves—and in healing and ritual. The ti plant has high mana and has thus been a favored tool of the kahuna for spiritual work. Like the kukui nut, it contains oils that can hold a charge of mana. In purification and blessing rituals that are still practiced today, a ti leaf is dipped into a mixture of water and olena and sprinkled throughout a dwelling. Hawaiians often surround their homes with ti plants to repel negative vibrations. When visiting Hawaii you can buy ti plant logs and grow them at home. The plants are sensitive to cold and make good indoor companions. Do not place them in the bedroom, however, as you may have trouble sleeping due to the energy they radiate.

HEALING

When the Basic Self feels stress, the brain sends the tension to a part of the body that corresponds to the kind of emotion being felt. With repeated stress and congestion, an energy block can develop in that area over time. A failure of love may affect the heart, for example, and failure to express emotional needs may lead to a throat problem. Many disease states can be traced back to a source in the Basic Self's way of thinking and feeling and a resulting energy block. Healing begins when the energy block is identified, the source is discovered, and the tension in that part of the body is relieved.

The gap between standard medicine and alternative medicine is narrowing. As millions of people use alternative methods of healing, the medical profession has begun to acknowledge the effectiveness of a variety of healing methods. This is entirely in line with the Huna approach. The kahuna of old Hawaii used every means possible to effect a cure and worked on many levels—spiritual, emotional, and physical. Modern society is rediscovering this holistic concept of healing.

When illness ensues, the Huna approach is to take advantage of everything and everyone at hand, including physicians, shamans, pharmacists, psychologists, Vector counselors, herbologists, acupuncturists, and hypnotherapists. At the first sign of sickness, go into the Silence and ask your Basic Self to give you answers about the root cause of your illness. You can dialogue directly with the afflicted part of the body since it is part of the Basic Self. Then ask the High Self for guidance and healing. The sooner you can do this, the faster you can begin the healing process. Visit a physician or other health professional to learn about the problem. Be very kind to your Basic Self and get lots of rest and good food. Gather and send mana to your High Self to assist in healing the body.

The Basic Self responds readily to physical action, so visiting health professionals makes a bold statement that you are concerned about your body's needs. Taking medication, herbs, and vitamins indicates to the Basic Self that you are taking steps to heal yourself. Medicines and herbs can change the physical vibration in a positive way that begins the healing process.

On a cautionary note, if you give the responsibility for your own health completely to a health professional, you will be subject to that person's thought patterns. An excellent book by two Huna practitioners in the medical profession, Allen and Lisa Lawrence, discusses the ways in which physicians can unknowingly perpetuate a belief in illness and implant negative suggestions in the patient's mind. The authors give an inspired account of how Huna can assist the individual in creating wellness.[20]

An independent approach is always best. In the Huna way, you work with the Selves to find the root cause of the disease and eliminate it. At the same time, you can work with a physician to alleviate the symptoms, and a hypnotist to uncover basic assumptions, while utilizing massage, diet, and vitamins to strengthen the body and get the mana flowing. You may gather mana and perform a Ha Rite and you may get together with other Huna practitioners to perform the Healing Circle ritual. It is never suggested that you use these as a substitute for medical help or medication. In Huna, you make use of every means of healing at your disposal.

Look to the kind of illness for a clue as to the emotional factor behind it. When you have any chronic illness or condition, look for a longstanding emotional problem. This may sound simplistic, but the Basic Self is simplistic. The complex chemical and bioenergetic powerhouse that is the human body can manifest marvelous health or dramatic illness, depending on the messages you send the Basic Self.

Many people who actively practice metaphysics feel ashamed and guilty when they manifest illness. They feel that in some way their metaphysics has failed them, and they may gloss over or cover up the disease that has overtaken them. Please do not add more blame and guilt to an already stressed-out Basic Self if illness comes to you. If the physical ailment is slight, go about your Huna business of looking for an emotional factor while using a holistic approach, and be thankful that you are being given an opportunity to head off a problem before it becomes serious.

If you should manifest a serious illness, do not blame yourself. Look on it as a challenge to learn about yourself and immediately begin to approach it from all sides. Communicate with your Basic Self, your High Self, your guides, and your physician. Write in your journal as a means of discovering your emotions. Look at what is not working in your entire life for clues. Is there a problem with your one-to-one relationship? Your daily job/activity? Are you suppressing your true nature? Are you getting on with your real aim in life? Do you need to move on to another phase of your life? Use all of this information to evaluate your emotional state. Believe that you have the power to change any physical condition. See your body as the dynamic, changeable, suggestible, marvelous piece of spirit/matter it is. Know that you have a blueprint in your aka body of your perfect body. Be aware that if you can eliminate the source of imbalance between the aka body and the physical body, the physical body can return to a state of health. Use the Silence, hoʻoponopono, and the Ha Rite to return the emotional and physical body to its optimum state.

It is another matter when a loved one becomes ill, and this person does not have knowledge of Huna, nor a desire to acquire it. Offer your help and information, but be aware that every person is walking her or his own path and may not be receptive to your suggestions. If you are unable to help with Huna healing, ask the person if you can pray for them. If you have their permission, do a Ha Rite and, in your next Huna group meeting, put them in the Healing Circle. Gather and direct mana to the High Self to use for whatever purpose is in their highest and best interest. In other words, let their own High Self determine the use of the mana you send.

One Huna student reported that her brother became seriously ill with a painful intestinal problem that landed him in the hospital. Naturally very distressed, she visited her brother and asked him if she could help him with healing, to which he assented, though he did not believe in any form of religious or spiritual intervention. That night, using her Huna techniques, she gathered mana and sent it to the High Self, asking that the mana be used to aid her brother in healing. When she visited him in the hospital the next day, he was much improved and out of pain. His condition worsened that night, and by the next day, he was suffering. The next night, the student did her ritual again, and the following day, the patient improved again. This happened several more times—she did the ritual, he improved, and then he worsened. She began to realize that her mana was alleviating his pain temporarily, but not eliminating the root cause of his problem. She then went into the Silence and called upon her High Self, asking it to communicate with her brother's High Self to provide information about the root cause of his illness. The answer from the High Self was simple. He was "doing too many things in his life that he didn't want to do."

After receiving this information, the student visited her brother in the hospital, and knowing that he wouldn't respond if she told him she had a message from his High Self, she approached him obliquely and gently. He was out of pain for the time being, though the doctors were talking about performing an operation since he wasn't improving. She told him that she had been thinking about him and believed there was a connection between his illness and his life. She asked him about his job and how things in his life were going. During their discussion, he identified one area of his life—his job—where he was performing work that he hated. She suggested that his "doing too many things he didn't want to do" might be contributing to his illness. To her surprise, he agreed, and they talked about his need for a change of job. In the next few days, his symptoms abated quickly, and he was able to go home. It seemed that this simple recognition on the conscious level had helped him alter the disease process. He had been enduring the hated job on the assumption that he would have a hard time finding another one. After a short while, however, he left the job and soon found another, more agreeable, means of employment.

A Hawaiian *kumu* (teacher), Abraham Kawai'i, once called the body "the filing cabinet of the mind," the sum of your experience and your emotion. The disease process, according to Kawai'i, is an accumulation process, and the healing process is a drainage process. This is true on the mental, spiritual, and physical levels. The key to healing, says Kawai'i, is release. Illness is a signal that things are out of balance in some area, and some issue needs to be addressed. Draining off negative emotions and basic assumptions is essential to this process. If the imbalance can be corrected on the emotional level, then the body can begin to heal.

Regarding "inherited" diseases, many people have an iron-clad belief that when something "runs in the family," it is inevitable. It seems perfectly reasonable to students of Huna that they can have an effect on their bodies in ridding themselves of illnesses, as long as the illnesses are not the inherited ones. So many people speak fatalistically of an illness or condition that has come down through generations and which they either have now or expect to have in the future. In the Huna system, no illness or condition is inevitable. People in families do tend to manifest the same physical problems because they are "like-minded"—their Basic Selves are sharing thoughts and emotions on a daily basis. It is not necessary to activate the disease-causing gene, however. Though many people in generations of your family have had diseases such as diabetes, heart attacks, or cancer, Huna teaches there is no reason for you to develop these. In some cases, because a family "shares" physical, mental, and emotional characteristics, there may be a tendency toward high cholesterol or low blood sugar. If you know this, you can work in advance on the basic assumptions that contribute to the problem. This presents a great opportunity to Huna practitioners to identify thought patterns in the family and to change the ones that produce illness.

Finally, in promoting healing on a daily basis, affirmations—positive statements that you make silently or verbally—are powerful tools. This signals your Basic Self of your intention to heal and to enjoy good health. You can do affirmations in general, such as, "I am feeling better all the time," or specific ones for any condition, such as, "My leg is healing and fast returning to normal." Visualize a picture of yourself in robust health while doing the affirmation to reinforce it. In the case of a leg injury, visualize yourself walking vigorously in one of your favorite nature settings. Don't wait until a problem worsens to do affirmations. As soon as a problem appears, begin affirming healing and a return to health. Be careful not to use words in your affirmation that refer to the illness or disease, and do not "program" the time it takes to heal. Don't ever make an illness or condition your own by saying, "I want *my* cold symptoms to disappear." It would be better to say, "The cold symptoms are fast disappearing. I am feeling better and better." Frame your affirmation in the same terms as your prayer-action, always remembering that the Basic Self takes things literally.

HO'OPONOPONO FOR TWO

The therapeutic process of ho'oponopono in the forms used by the family and the individual has been described in the chapter on Practice. A modified process can be used to resolve problems between two persons, providing both agree to submit to it in a spirit of openness and goodwill. There obviously must be recognition by both that a problem exists and a sincere desire to resolve the difficulty.

In the "couples' ho'oponopono," one person calls for the session in order to address a certain problem. If the other person agrees, they decide on a place and time. There should be enough time and a place free of distractions. Begin the session with a prayer. If you want to use a Huna prayer, ask that your High Selves be present, along with all of your guides, angels, and guardians, and that your Basic Selves fully assist you in the process. Agree ahead of time not to speak in angry voices, but to speak calmly, and to let the other speak without interruption. Agree not to say things that might hurt one another.

The person who called the session speaks first without interruption for about five minutes. She (she/he is used arbitrarily here) states the nature of the problem as she understands it and says why she wants to have it examined and resolved. When she is finished speaking, she signals she is done, and the other person begins speaking for about five minutes, uninterrupted. He states his understanding of the problem, signaling when he is done. Then, she speaks again for five minutes, focusing on her own involvement in the problem. He speaks again, identifying further aspects of the problem, focusing on his own involvement only. After both have finished speaking on their own, discussion is permitted.

The next step is sharing of feelings, again in turn—how this problem made both feel, and how both would prefer to feel about it. Honesty and openness are valuable during this part of the process. The next step is a crucial one. Each person states how they contributed to creating the problem and how they can contribute to resolving it. The discussion next addresses steps they both might take to resolve and release the problem. The two come to an agreement about definite actions to be taken in the future.

The person who called the session then summarizes what has occurred, and how the problem is going to be addressed and resolved. The two state their commitment to the relationship and to living in harmony. There is a closing prayer and if desired, a sharing of food.

If this sounds too idyllic, be assured that it works well as long as the two people involved agree to abide by the rules and continue the process through to the end. Though hoʻoponopono can be used to resolve many kinds of problems, do not feel that it has to be something momentous. For example, one couple had been car hunting for a month and both were becoming frustrated at not being able to agree on a car to buy. They finally held a "car hoʻoponopono," conducted by the above rules, during which they discovered that they each wanted a completely different kind of car. Out of courtesy they had been test driving the cars the other was interested in, and no decision was ever reached. When they both truly expressed their feelings about what they wanted in a car, they were able to reach an agreement as to what to look for. They brought home a car they were both happy with that same weekend.

HOUSE GUARDIANS

The Hawaiian kahuna often placed two wooden figures of deities at the entrance to their dwelling. The figures, made of hardwood, were charged with mana and protected against negativity entering the home. You can charge a figure or object with mana from the High Self to be kept either outside or inside your home. Choose any figure that resonates with your spirit or simply use an abstract wooden shape. Two figures work even better.

Upright stones also make excellent guardians. Always ask permission before moving a stone from its location in nature. Choose stones that have high mana, and let the stones tell you which ones would work best for your purpose. Gather mana and offer it to the stone to make it even more powerful.

HULA

Hawaiian hula is a sacred dance with ancient origins. Performed by both men and women, it was, and is, a way of invoking the gods and connecting with the power of nature. Its graceful, dynamic movements exemplify the expression of the vital life force and are both centering and balancing. Over the centuries, hula has been used in a variety of ways, as ritual, as celebration, and as communication with the gods. Chants that accompany hula use the powerful dimension of sound to raise the mana of the dancers.

Today, hula sometimes takes the form of entertainment, but whether you are drawn to see hula or to practice it, search out *hula kahiko* (ancient hula), which is the form that relates most closely to Huna. Should you wish to study hula, find a *kumu hula* (hula teacher or master) and give your Basic Self the joy of practicing this ancient form of spirituality.

HUNA GROUPS

Once you have integrated Huna techniques and ideas into your life, you might want to practice with a group. Groups generally create higher energy levels than one individual can achieve, and raising mana together is powerful. You can pool your mana to direct it to a shared goal or focus it on individual needs, or both. You can also bring others into the group for education about Huna and discussion of aspects of Huna.

Form a group of like-minded persons to meet periodically to gather mana, do prayer-actions, and share information. You can begin by studying texts or proceeding through the lessons published by Huna Research Inc. (see Appendix), or going through a Huna book chapter by chapter, with or without a leader. You can watch a videotape or listen to an audiotape of Huna together. Discuss the subject afterwards. After the basics of Huna have been mastered, choose a subject to explore each meeting, such as ho'oponopono or the Ha Rite, and both discuss it and put it into practice.

At the beginning of each meeting, hold a meditation in which you go into the Silence and gather mana to offer to the High Self. At the end of the meeting, go into the Silence and gather mana again. Form a Healing Circle with everyone in the group in which you gather mana and send it to the High Selves of all of those present as well as those known to you who need and want healing. While in the circle, have each participant repeat the first names of those to whom the mana is being directed (see Rituals).

Make the meetings fun—you always want to appeal to the Basic Self in your activities—by including food, flowers, and Hawaiian music. Occasionally, invite Hawaiians from your area to give demonstrations of hula and chanting. Once your group is established, plan to attend a Huna gathering given by one of the Huna organizations or create your own outing.

INSOMNIA

Sleep is a complex state that involves both the Middle Self and Basic Self in different ways. It is the Middle Self that sleeps while the Basic Self conditions the body for the sleep state and then keeps watch over bodily functions. Normally, when it is time for sleep, your body and mind relax together, and sleep ensues. When your Basic Self is worried or anxious about something, however, the body becomes tense, and the waking state is retained. Put another way, the Basic Self needs help with the "trouble," and since the Middle Self is the problem solver, the Basic Self keeps the Middle Self awake or wakes it up after the body has slept for an hour or two. The body is tense and anxious, tossing and turning, while the mind tries to apply logic to solve the problem. In its tired state, the Middle Self is unable to think clearly, because its thoughts are intermingled with anxiety feelings from the Basic Self. The result is worry insomnia, characterized by the frustrated attempts of the Middle Self to "do something" about the Basic Self's anxiety in the middle of the night.

Worry insomnia can be the Basic Self's way of communicating to the Middle Self that there is a problem that is not being addressed during waking hours. Perhaps the Basic Self is disturbed by an incident—something that was done, or said—during the day, or perhaps by an ongoing difficulty. Perhaps the Middle Self hasn't found this worthy of attention, but the Basic Self feels differently. The Basic Self wants you to deal with the problem.

In this form of insomnia, whether you have difficulty going to sleep or you wake up in the middle of the night and can't go back to sleep, it is helpful to identify as soon as possible the source of your Basic Self's anxiety. Of course, you may know what it is already, but it is still helpful to hear it from your Basic

Self. Lying in bed with your eyes closed, take several slow, measured breaths, and begin dialoguing with your Basic Self:

"My wonderful Basic Self, I love you. I can feel that you are tense and worried. Please tell me why." Listen for an answer, and notice any thoughts and pictures that you have immediately after asking. Frame the anxiety in a few sentences, such as, "You are angry about what happened today at work with Terry. You are still upset. You are worried about how we can deal with it." Once the source of anxiety is identified, reassure your Basic Self, "My dear Basic Self: I understand your anger and anxiety, and I'm sorry I did not see this before. We cannot solve this problem now. Sleep is important to refresh us, and we need to sleep. I promise you that we will work together to solve this problem tomorrow. Please be assured, all will be well. We know we can solve any problem that comes to us. Peace, now. Peace. Peace." Take several more slow, measured breaths. Send loving thoughts to your Basic Self and flood your mind with a soft, rose pink light.

When you make a promise like this to your Basic Self, you must keep it. The Basic Self remembers and will not take your promises seriously in the future if you renege on the ones you make. The following morning, sit down as soon as possible with a sheet of paper and jot down your understanding of the problem with your co-worker. Write down three things you can do to make the situation better. Act on those that very day.

Sometimes you need only comfort the Basic Self and assure it that all is well. One student told of the following incident: One evening, her neighbor was burning some yard debris next door. Since she lived in a rural area where this was often done, she was not too concerned, though it was the dry season and fires had been prohibited. Before going to bed, she worried a little that the fire might not have been put out properly and would rekindle in the warm night breeze. She went to sleep but woke up about 2:00 A.M. When she asked her Basic Self what the matter was, the reply was "Check on the fire." Her Basic Self had registered her concern and had duly awakened her for the purpose of checking on things. She went to the window and found there was no fire, so reassured her Basic Self that they were safe and could now go back to sleep. She also gave her Basic Self the suggestion that she did not need to "check on the fire" any more that night.

Another form of insomnia occurs when your Middle Self—your thinking mind—has been overstrained, such as when you work late and then go straight to bed. You may experience the feeling of not being able to "turn your mind off" in order to relax. Your Middle Self has been running on reserves of mana and needs to let go of its demands on the body's mana. Do the following exercise: First, clear your mind of all the thoughts by pushing them off the mind's center stage and visualizing nothing—just hold in your mind a blank space, filled with color if you wish. Say to your Basic Self: "My dear Basic Self. I am clearing away all the thoughts I have at this time and giving this entire body completely to your care. Please be in charge now." See your thoughts dissolving into nothingness and see only space where they were. You are voluntarily disengaging your Middle Self and allowing your Basic Self to be in charge of the body. Many people report that they fall asleep instantly with this technique.

JOY OF LIFE

Life was not meant to be a grim affair. A sea of joy exists beneath the surface of reality, waiting for the person with awareness to tap into it. The ancient Hawaiians celebrated their gods with feasting, chants, and hula. Modern Hawaiians still gather to feast, make music, sing, perform hula and chants, surf, canoe race, and just "talk story." The goal of all Huna practice is to savor existence joyfully while expressing who you are. Consider what you love to do on both the Basic and Middle Self levels and make time for those as well as spending time with friends and being in nature. Remember the concept of balance between the material and spiritual when allocating your time. Leave time for joy.

LIVELIHOOD

A job is a vehicle for playing out your thought patterns in the world. Whether you are overworked, stressed, underpaid, or in harmony with your employment, all of these patterns are coming through your thoughts and manifesting in outside reality. In order to change your experience of your employment, then, it is necessary to change your thought patterns. If you are stressed, then you are manifesting a belief in stress and the idea that life is difficult. If you are underpaid, your thought patterns reflect a lack of self-worth.

174

Decide what it is that you want to change in your employment. Look for patterns in past jobs you've had, such as overbearing supervisors, taking on too much work, being usurped by a co-worker, or lacking creativity in your work. Admit to yourself that this is not coming to you from outside but is emanating from you and your ideas about yourself and the world.

Once you have identified these, work on the problems individually with your Basic and High Selves in the Silence. Write down a scenario of the perfect job for you and read it to the universe. Gather mana and offer it to the High Self in order to bring harmony to your current job or to manifest another job. Do this as often as needed until your situation changes.

A job is also a way of manifesting your purpose. So many people search for something to do that will magically transform their lives into a meaningful existence. In truth, all existence is meaningful, and whatever you do on a daily basis has value. Rather than seek a life path outside of yourself, work instead on freeing your Selves from harmful patterns and on building your mana so that you can realize your dreams. When you are free from fear and have all Three Selves working together in harmony, life's exciting possibilities open up to you.

LOVING THE BASIC SELF

As you get comfortable dialoguing with your Basic Self, you will also become more sensitive to what gives your Basic Self joy and happiness. When you are considerate of your Basic Self, your Basic Self will reciprocate when you ask it to do something difficult for you. One of the ways you can interact with the Basic Self is through color.

Color

Colors have an effect on the Basic Self whether you are aware of it or not. Learning to use color consciously can enhance your Basic Self's functioning and build a bridge between the Middle and Basic Selves. For example, before getting dressed in the morning, ask your Basic Self what colors would be beneficial to wear that day. Which metals or gemstones would be optimal? People often make these decisions intuitively—at the Basic Self level—but it works even better if you do it with both intuition and consciousness. Although color is an individual thing, you can use the following as general guidelines for working with color.

Amber infuses the aura with radiance and warmth.

Blue promotes deep thinking and meditative states. Light blue is gentle and soothing. Navy blue and lapis promote attention to the job at hand and encourage discipline. Indigo links the soul with the God realm.

Brown lowers the vibration. When brown is combined with white–as on *tapa* cloth–it is warmer and therefore becomes centering and grounding.

Gold raises the overall vibration and energy and increases abundance consciousness.

Green assists in healing the body and dispels a poverty mentality. A true emerald green is best for this purpose.

176

Forest green helps you rest mentally. Light green or lime promotes optimism and helps you look forward to a bright future. Avocado green helps you speak your truth and be outgoing and assertive.

Orange is a stimulating, clarifying color to the Basic Self.

Pink is the vibration of love. It strengthens your willingness to love and be loved. Pink coral is balancing.

Purple raises the spiritual vibration. Deep purple gives you spiritual strength. Lilac connects you with higher powers and unseen forces. Magenta encourages deep spiritual healing.

Red stimulates the Basic Self and enhances energy and sexuality. Red can be intensely positive or intensely negative. Ruby red raises physical energy. Light red clarifies the emotions.

Silver transforms negativity and keeps the mind elevated.

Turquoise is a universally uplifting color that neutralizes negative energy while it provides grounding on the physical level.

Yellow gathers together disparate energy and scattered thought patterns.

Black and *White* are subject to the intention of the individual. In general, wearing black protects the Basic Self from overstimulation from the outside (which is why it's worn a lot in cities), and white expands the sense of self.

Combinations of colors can be very effective:

Blue and red aids in accomplishment on the physical plane (work-related, material, financial). These are good colors to wear when starting a new business or enterprise.

Gold and silver combines spirituality with physical grounding and is a powerful combination in both colors and metals.

Green and gold manifests abundance.

Pink and green promotes loving in a responsible way.

Purple and green encourages feelings of happiness and sensuality.

Red and green is a statement of individuality and brings balance to the physical body.

Red and yellow indicate boldness and power. These were the colors of the Hawaiian *ali'i* or royalty.

A general guideline for clothing is to avoid muddy colors—those in which different colors have been mixed to excess—and to have a repertoire of colors that you love in your closet for different needs.

Color can also provide a key to your energy level and your mental state. If you find yourself choosing black a lot, you may be overstimulated by the outside world. Pay attention to your Basic Self's need to spend time alone and rest. If you choose red often, your physical energy may be low because you are trying to do too many things. Work at simplifying your schedule and building your mana.

When choosing colors for your clothes or your home, ignore what is in fashion and select what pleases you. Involve your Basic Self in the decision. When decorating your home, avoid wall colors that are too stimulating to the Basic Self, and rather choose gentle colors that promote a sense of comfort and rest. To add excitement to a room where social activities take place, display colorful art works. Always be aware that your Basic Self is affected by what it sees on a daily basis. Surround yourself with positive visions that speak to your soul.

Food

Being conscious of what you eat is an important way to show your Basic Self that you care. With food, you transform matter into mana. Thus, it stands to reason that the quality of the food you eat affects the quality of the energy you gather and manifest. There is no right or wrong way to eat. It is entirely individual. When you tune into the Basic Self's reactions to foods, you will discover those that are optimum for you.

For example, a woman who had always liked chocolate and who had grown up eating chocolate candy and ice cream, resolved to become more conscious of her body's reactions to foods. She began paying attention to how she felt after eating and made a startling discovery: every time she ate chocolate, she experienced nasal congestion and a mild headache. She was clearly allergic to the substance. At first, she was dismayed to find that something she liked could cause an adverse reaction. It was confusing as well. She wondered why she had been eating chocolate all her life. Actually, her Basic Self had been conditioned early in life by others to like the taste of chocolate even though the substance wasn't compatible with her body. She had simply ignored the reaction because she wasn't conscious of it and knew others around her loved chocolate. Once she— the Middle Self—understood the effect chocolate had on her, she began to avoid it. To her Middle Self's amazement, the Basic Self cooperated in the decision. She learned to substitute other flavors that the Basic Self liked but that did not cause her to have an allergic reaction.

Once you begin to listen to your Basic Self, you will likely discover that you are eating things that are not compatible with your body. You may also find that you are not eating things that your Basic Self needs. When your Middle Self and Basic Self work together to make food choices, your body benefits, and food can take its rightful place in your life as a joyous, life-giving experience.

Creative Expression

Think of how children love to paint, dance, sing, and run. When the child becomes an adult, these activities are often put away as "childish things." In order to be a joyful human being, the Basic Self needs an outlet of expression that bypasses the Middle Self. This does not mean that thinking and planning are not involved, only that the activity be creative and spontaneous. Let your Basic Self choose the means of expression: noncompetitive sports, arts, dance, music, or just walking in nature may fill the Basic Self's need for expression. In a dialogue, ask your Basic Self what it wants to do. Start simply, and do not place agendas on the activity. In other words, if you want to do art, don't think in terms of becoming a famous artist and selling your work for lots of money. Just let the Basic Self do what it wants to do for a change, just for the joy of it.

Monitoring
One of the kindest things you can do for your Basic Self is to monitor what it sees and hears on a daily basis. Movies, television, books, and newspapers all have a powerful effect on the Basic Self, and their input can live in the memory for years. When you expose the Basic Self to too much negative input from the outside world, anxiety may be the result. One man had a habit of watching the late news before he went to bed every night. When he became more conscious of his Basic Self, he realized that he was exposing it to a negatively stimulating half hour of shootings, accidents, fires, and other mayhem right before going to sleep. He stopped his late news habit and found he slept better and had a better outlook on life.

In general, when you are reading a book or watching a movie or show on television, ask yourself, does this serve my highest good? If not, walk away. "Highest good" can include a wide spectrum of different things: spiritual growth, wisdom, knowledge, curiosity, diversion, or pure rollicking entertainment. If none of these needs are being served in an optimum way, end your involvement. Leave the theater, close the book, turn off the television.

MANIFESTING

You can manifest many things in your life with the following technique:

1. State firmly what you want when you are in a happy, clear mood.

2. Hold your concentration on the goal with a clear picture. See it in your mind's eye, and do not change the picture while working on it.

3. Release all resistance and negativity within yourself to it.

4. Make certain it does not affect other people.

5. Feel that you already have it and visualize this state of being. Imagine how you would feel if you had money, had health, had energy, had success, etc.

6. Gather mana by deep breathing.

7. Ask your Basic Self to cooperate with you in bringing the mana to your High Self in order to realize your goal.

8. Never question how it will be given to you and never doubt that it will come to you.

9. Do not tell anyone else what you are working on. When you tell others who are not supportive, their negative feelings and doubts could affect the outcome.

10. Know that there is an infinite supply of everything you need in the universe and that you can draw it to you.

MASSAGE

More and more, massage is being recognized for its value as a complementary means of healing the body. The Hawaiians used a form of deep tissue massage called *lomilomi* as a very effective healing practice. Lomilomi is still practiced today and takes various forms depending on the practitioner. Along with relieving muscle tension, this kind of massage often has a spiritual dimension. It can involve bathing, heat application, herbs, chants, and affirmations. Some practitioners do not touch the patient and work on the patient's energy field with their hands. As a Huna practice, lomilomi is a way of imparting mana to the person for healing while manipulating the body to cause mana to flow more readily. Deep relaxation allows the body to build the mana it needs to heal.

NAME POWER

People often ignore the obvious in their search for truth— their names. With a good naming dictionary, study the definition of all of your names—your family, given, married, and nicknames. Then, look for inner meanings in them that give you a clue to your path in life.

Names were very important to the Hawaiians, and a child might be given a mystical name by a kahuna, a family member, or even a god. This name was a treasured personal possession that could not be used without permission. Names could be changed if the person's current energy required a new name.

Meditate on your name and see if you can discover its mystical meanings for yourself. If you want to bring a certain quality into your life, select a mystical name that only you know that embodies this quality (or ask a spiritual guide or advisor to give you one). Grant others permission to use the name if this feels right.

OMENS AND SIGNS

The ancient Hawaiians looked for signs in nature and took these and other omens very seriously. Cloud formations and other manifestations of weather, the appearance of the ocean, animals encountered along a path or heard at night, movements and aspects of the moon, stars, and planets, or the behavior of birds or fish all had meaning and were subject to interpretation. Anything out of the ordinary might portend an event that was to happen or had already happened. The appearance of a rainbow, for example, could indicate something momentous of either a positive or negative nature.

When working with your own signs and omens, notice anything unusual that comes across your path and interpret it according to what is going on in your life. One Huna student had made a spiritual journey to Hawaii and was working happily with a teacher there. They were driving back late at night after visiting the volcano when a Hawaiian owl *(pueo)* swooped in front of the car and proceeded ahead of them. The owl in Hawaii is associated with the *aumakua* or ancestral spirit, and the two regarded this as a highly positive omen that they were on the right track and were being guided in their

184

work by a higher wisdom. The training continued and concluded successfully.

Understand that wisdom can come from many sources, and that your High Self may work through different phenomena to send you a message. The message may come from a friend, or a stranger, an animal, and even television or the radio. Learn to be sensitive to what is going on around you, and the answers will emerge. If you feel spiritual kinship with a particular animal or form of life—a tree, a bird, a plant—or with an element— wind, clouds, the ocean—spend time in their presence and seek your answers there. Know that no wisdom is deliberately obscured from you, and that you can have access to higher insight if you make yourself open to it.

PEACEFUL MIND

Most people pursue happiness and peace of mind from the standpoint of not having them. Actually, having a happy attitude and a peaceful state of mind creates a powerful mana field that affects every aspect of life and attracts positive mana to you. Practice being happy and peaceful first, and the attributes of a happy life will follow. When you are taking steps to manifest something, only work on it when you are in a happy, positive mood, because your mood colors how it will turn out. If you are anxious while you work at manifesting, your final result will have a flaw in it. Practice having a day-to-day peaceful, happy energy that flows into every aspect of your life.

PENDULUM P3RACTICE

The pendulum is an excellent device for communicating with your Basic Self, though not all Basic Selves like using it. Work with it for a while to see if it suits you. If it does, you will have an effective means of accessing your Basic Self any time and any place.

You can buy a pendulum in a metaphysical store or make your own by suspending an object on a chain or string. Be sure the weight is balanced. Begin by instructing your Basic Self in the signals. Teach your Basic Self that when the pendulum swings in a forward and backward motion, this signifies "yes." When it swings from side to side, this is a "no." When it swings in a circle, this means, "I don't know." Swing the pendulum forwards and backwards intentionally, letting your Basic Self know that this is a yes answer. Then, swing it sideways to demonstrate a no answer. Questions, obviously, should be only those that can be answered by yes or no.

It is important, when asking questions of the Basic Self, to only ask for information that the Basic Self can provide. Do not ask about the future or about issues that are too complex.

To begin using the pendulum, go into the Silence and maintain a quietly receptive state. Hold the chain attached to the pendulum in one hand. To get the Basic Self used to this dialogue, ask the Basic Self a few things you are pretty sure you already know the answer to, such as "Do you like chocolate?" Hold the chain steady and let the pendulum move completely on its own. When you are satisfied that you are getting correct answers, progress to real questions. Once your Basic Self has become used to communicating in this way, you can use the pendulum to obtain a wealth of feedback and helpful information.

POSSESSION

Possession, or *noho,* of the living body by a spirit, was well known to the Hawaiians, and there are many references to it in Hawaiian lore. A person could be possessed by an ancestor or by a disembodied spirit sent by a kahuna. Max Freedom Long referred to "eating companions" that attached themselves to the aura and stole vital life force from living beings.

Some of the conditions that make a person vulnerable to spirit possession or influence are the following: alcohol intoxication, drug and tranquilizer use, frequent negative thinking and speaking, guilt and sin complexes, and physical and mental exhaustion. In order to guard against possession or influence, do the following:

1. Think and speak positively.

2. Cut ties to negative people.

3. Abstain from alcohol and drugs and avoid bars.

4. Remove guilt and sin complexes from the Basic Self.

5. Forgive yourself and others.

6. Take hot baths with a pinch of salt charged with mana from the High Self.

7. Spend time in nature.

8. Keep physical strength high with nourishing food,

vitamins, and exercise. Drink lots of water. Breathe deeply to increase mana.

9. Repeat positive affirmations such as: "I am free and my mana is strong," or "I am the living presence of God."

10. Wear red coral around your neck.

A person in good health who thinks and acts positively is not in any great danger of possession, though well-meaning relatives who have passed on may linger around and in the aura. The best way to avoid influence or intrusion is to keep your mana high, rid your Basic Self of complexes and negativity, and stay in close touch with the High Self. If you suspect that you or someone you know may be possessed or influenced, seek the help of a Huna practitioner or an experienced exorcist. Jack Gray, Huna teacher and a well-known exorcist, believed it was not enough to rid the person of the possessing entity, but to work with the problem that caused the possession in the first place. His condition for conducting an exorcism was that he be allowed to teach the possessed person—as well as the invading entity—Huna.

RECONNECTING WITH THE EARTH

In the spring of 1980, a young Hawaiian navigator, Nainoa Thompson, guided a sixty-foot canoe from Hawaii to Tahiti and back, a total distance of over 4,000 miles. He used no instruments. He was accompanied by Mau Piailug, a native of Satawal, who had made a similar pioneering journey in 1976. Both men navigated by minute observation of the stars and the sun, the ocean waves, swells, and currents, and other natural phenomena. In navigating in this manner, they emulated the methods of their voyaging Polynesian ancestors who crossed thousands of miles of open ocean to populate far-flung islands. This was one of the best examples the world has ever known of humans interacting with the natural world.

Today, modern society has caused some people to lose connection with their source. The body has its own natural rhythms that are independent of the clock that usually dictates its schedule. Hours are spent at desks and computers in rooms illuminated by fluorescent lights. Air is conditioned. Estrangement from natural surroundings has almost become the norm.

Take time to reconnect. Spend a short time each day in the following activities which can be done by anyone on any schedule. Many of them can be combined.

Silence

The sounds of machines are everywhere—the roar of distant freeways, the drone of planes, the hum of household appliances. In the midst of this din, which is often taken for granted, it is important to have some silence. Find the quietest place you can, inside or out-of-doors, and make yourself comfortable. Concentrate on the silence. Let sounds and thoughts flow by. If you are indoors, it may help to visualize a place of serenity such as a pond in the forest or a cloud-swept mountaintop. Give yourself completely to silence. Do this for a few minutes each day.

Listening

The earth is speaking constantly. Spend a few minutes every day simply listening to all the sounds around you. Hear the machine sounds and separate them out. Then, listen to the voices of the earth: the cry of a bird, the chattering of a squirrel, the whispering of the wind, the sound of rain. Throughout your day, listen for natural sounds. After a while, you will discover subtle patterns that emerge from them. Become sensitive to nature's signs. Let the cries of seabirds foretell rain. Let crickets tell you the temperature.

Outside

The natural world is a tremendous source of mana. Spend time out-of-doors every day, even if it's only half an hour. Rearrange your day to include a walk, a lunch hour excursion, or time to just sit under a tree. When you feel in a negative mood, getting outdoors is even more important. Spend time near trees, rocks, and water. The Basic Self needs time outside in nature.

Close observation

Choose a natural spot and visit it often. Closely observe its features—the form of a tree, the shape of a rock, the colors, the insects, the feeling of the air. Over time, observe the changes that occur on a minute level. It's fun to keep a diary of the place and record your observations in it.

Grounding

Find a spot of earth. Place your hands on it. Feel that you are fully connected to the planet. Feel yourself on top of this great round ball, and reflect that this is the same earth surface that stretches across continents. Picture the crust of the earth and the fiery core beneath. Know that you are of this earth. Its minerals are in your body, and its seawater flows through your veins. Its rhythms echo in your longings. The earth is your birthright.

Daily rhythms

Become aware of the rhythms of the day and night and how they affect you. Learn when you function best. If you haven't been outside to see a sunrise in a long time, plan a time when you can rise early and greet the day. Do this at least once a month. During the day, notice the position of the sun and the quality of the light. At sundown, pause to watch the light leave the earth. Become aware of the phases of the moon and notice their effects on you.

Seasons

The Hawaiians had a period of renewal called the *Makahiki* when work was kept at a minimum, and all warfare ceased. The normal religious observances were not required. Games were played and people spent their time at leisure and sports, often visiting friends in other locales. The Makahiki began in late fall and lasted about three months.

Although you probably can't take a three months' holiday, you can develop your own sensitive relationship to the seasons. This may require some adjustment. When nature's energy decreases as it does during the fall, society demands that you "gear up"—go back to school, intensify work after the vacation, and begin regular activities again. This is opposite to nature and likely the reason why there is so much sickness in early winter. During fall, it would serve you better to gradually begin decreasing your activities. By midwinter, humans need to be, like the rest of nature, taking it easy. Spring is the time for beginning new projects, and summer the time to put them into action. Throughout the year, be aware that the amount of light indicates the amount of energy available to you in nature.

Another way of reconnecting is to keep a weather diary of your area, recording natural events and conditions of the seasons. Pay attention to the summer and winter solstices, which are special times of the year. At those times, nature's energy changes, and this affects everyone, whether they are aware of it or not.

Scents

One of our most sensitive faculties is mostly unused. Retrieve your sense of smell. Become aware of the multitude of scents in your world and experience them consciously. For one day, focus on all the smells around you. Notice the ways in which your behavior relates to the smells you encounter in your environment.

Unclothed

Spending so much time in clothes causes people to forget the beauty of their bodies and the place of the human body in the natural order. Whenever possible, spend ten minutes without clothes, apart from bathing and sleeping, simply being without clothes. Enjoy the feeling of lightness that comes from not being confined in coverings. Be aware of your amazing body as a finely wrought creation, your own unique part of physical existence.

Animal watching

Spend time with an animal, domestic or wild, focusing on its world. Forget your preconceived notions about the animal, and look at things through its eyes. Feel vicariously the joyful leap that begins your dog's day, the thrill your cat feels when chasing a ball. Watch squirrels cavort in trees or rabbits hop around in a field. See the world in the simple terms of an animal: food, security, comfort, play, love.

Doing nothing

Spend some time each day, preferably out-of-doors, doing nothing. Don't exercise, garden, read, or think. Empty your mind as much as possible and just be. Feel yourself existing.

RETURN TO THE SOURCE: HAWAII

For students of Huna, a trip to Hawaii is thrilling and rewarding. To experience Hawaii in all of its contrasts—the high mana of the ocean, the power of the volcano, the mystical sense of beauty, and the gentle spirit of aloha—is to know the essence of Huna. There are sacred sites and places of legend and antiquity on all the islands as well as dramatic and luxuriant manifestations of nature. There is the opportunity to see hula and hear Hawaiian chants and eat Hawaiian foods. Hawaii's incomparable people and the mix of cultures is like nowhere else on earth.

Before going to Hawaii, read as much as you can about the islands' history, cultures, mythology, and archaeology. That way, you will be able to see and experience it in all of its complexity. Hawaii is a complex place with rich, deep wellsprings that come not from mainstream America but from the ancient Pacific cultures. When traveling there, look beneath the surface of the resort society and you will find a vibrant and compelling way of life that is completely unique.

Hawaii is a place of healing and abundant mana, which is why so many people are drawn to it for rest and recreation. It has another aspect, too, which the casual visitor may not notice immediately. Hawaii clarifies and enhances energy. Whatever energy you bring with you (and whatever harmony or disharmony) will manifest and may be accentuated. It is a good idea, therefore, before your trip, to spend time clarifying your intention. On what level do you wish to experience Hawaii? Lightly? Deeply? Do you wish to experience relaxation and rejuvenation? Do you want to make a spiritual connection? Perhaps you want to be an adventurer and explorer? Ask your High Self for assistance and ask that Pele give you guidance on your journey.

Hawaii's major islands provide a wide spectrum of possibilities. Formed during different time periods and subject to different histories, the Hawaiian Islands all have their own special energies and personalities. Over time, people often develop an affinity for one island, but all are exciting places to visit. There are heiau (temples), sacred stones, petroglyphs, waterfalls, cultural sites, and natural wonders surrounded by sea and sky.

Because of its active volcano, Hawaii island—the Big Island—is a natural destination for students of Huna. Both sides of the island contain significant sites, and the best itinerary, if time permits, is one that circles the island. On the Hilo side, students of Huna should spend time in Hawaii Volcanoes National Park and see Kilauea Caldera and Halemaumau Crater, Pele's sacred home. North of Hilo, Akaka Falls, a 422-foot waterfall that plunges into a gorge below, and Kahuna Falls, located downstream, both surrounded by lush vegetation, have mythic significance. The cave behind beautiful Rainbow Falls, located in Wailuku River State Park, is the legendary home of the goddess Hina. On the Kona side, Puʻuhonua o Honaunau, or Place of Refuge, on Honaunau Bay, provided sanctuary for kapu breakers and defeated warriors. Today, the heiau, Hale o Keawe, surrounded by wood carvings of guardian deities, is still a powerful place with a strong aura of the past. Along the Kohala coast, the Puako petroglyph fields—an extensive area of lava rock with carvings of figures and symbols that you approach through a *kiawe* forest—is both intriguing and mysterious. On the coast are several important heiaus: Puʻukohola, built by King Kamehameha I in the late eighteenth century, is a National Historic Site, which can be viewed but not entered, and Moʻokini Luakini, a much older site, is a National Historic Landmark. Lapakahi State Historical Park, a reconstructed 600-year-old Hawaiian village right on the ocean, is educational and allows you to experience a piece of historical Hawaii.

Kauai is a spiritual island of stunning beauty, and the most ancient of the six major islands. Its eroded peaks covered with mist and its luxuriant vegetation epitomize a spiritual paradise. Kokee State Park is especially captivating, and Waimea Canyon is an awe-inspiring manifestation of nature. Kauai has some of Hawaii's most beautiful beaches, as well as an overall feeling of the sacred. Oahu, the most populous island, has a wealth of history and culture, and an international mix of peoples. In Honolulu, the Bishop Museum, with its excellent exhibits and displays of artifacts, gives you a glimpse into Hawaii's past as well as other related Pacific cultures. Near Honolulu, an easy hike that begins inside Diamond Head Crater (its Hawaiian name is Leʻahi), an extinct volcano and national natural landmark, is highly recommended. On the north shore of the island, which has a very different feeling from busy Honolulu, beautiful Waimea Falls Park has interesting archaeological sites and gardens. The less visited, relatively isolated island of Molokai had a reputation for being the last bastion for kahuna practices as well as sorcery and still retains the mystical feeling of old Hawaii. Molokai is a splendid island for walking and meditating and has a quality of intimacy and timelessness.

Maui has many sacred sites and a number of varied, exquisite terrains. In the West Maui Mountains, the Iao Valley, with its phallic Iao Needle, was a sacred place of rituals, burials, and sanctuary. Spectacular Haleakala Crater, "House of the Sun," in East Maui's Haleakala National Park, is formed from two dormant volcanoes that dominate the island's geography. It is a spiritual place of legend and otherworldliness. The beautiful and twisty Hana Highway takes you alongside waterfalls and verdant hidden grottoes. The formerly kapu Seven Pools at Ohe'o Gulch have a mystical beauty about them.

These are a just a few of the many places in Hawaii that students of Huna will find rewarding. When visiting a sacred site or heiau in Hawaii, approach it with respect and reverence. Tune in to the energies of the place and feel the presence of the sacred. Never take anything from a site. Leave an offering of a lei if you wish.

RITUALS

Rituals are focused, effective behaviors that are time-tested and known to achieve definite results. With their use of dramatic elements, they are an excellent way of impressing the Basic Self with the need for change and the fact that you are serious about it. Never do a ritual in the presence of a negative or skeptical person, for this person will drain energy from the ritual.

Healing Circle

In this ritual, you and others come together for the purpose of requesting healing from the High Selves. In a sense, what you are really asking is that the High Self balance the individual and provide her/him with the means to heal, in whatever form that may take. You may ask for healing for yourself, for others if you have permission, and for situations, places, and conflicts.

Like many rituals, this one is best done in the evening, in a quiet, congenial place among people of like mind.

For the setting, create an altar in the middle of the room with tapa or cloth, ti leaves or pine boughs, candles, flowers, and crystals, and ask participants to place personal objects (preferably of wood or metal, except watches) on the altar for the duration of the ceremony. This will imbue the objects with mana that will be created during the ritual. While people are quietly forming into a circle around the altar, set the mood with a tape of a Hawaiian chant, Hawaiian music, or other balancing, soothing music.

To begin, do a chant, shake a rattle, blow a conch, or beat a drum. This changes the atmosphere and announces that the ritual has begun. To begin the ritual, the designated leader says, "We are gathered tonight for the purpose of healing mind, spirit, and body, for ourselves, for others, and for the planet. Our means will be the methods of Huna, which we will use to gather and direct mana, or vital life force. We work on the belief that we are all healers, that we all have access to mana, and that we all can send and receive mana.

"Tonight we ask for healing with the awareness that illness is a message and an opportunity for learning about ourselves. We take responsibility for our own growth, for removing our blocks, and for bringing our lives into balance so that healing can take place. We ask healing for others only with their permission and at the level of the High Self.

"We ask that the High Selves of everyone in this room be present, and that the Po'e Aumakua, or Great Company of High

Selves, assist us. We sincerely ask the cooperation of all of the Basic Selves in this room. In order to bring in the High Selves, we will chant slowly, eight times, AU-MA-KUA." (The chant can be accompanied by the rattle or drum).

The leader then instructs: "Everyone in the circle link hands together and close your eyes. Take a series of sixteen slow, deep mana breaths at your own pace, building the mana slowly. Visualize a huge force of mana being created within the circle, and as you continue to breathe, picture it intensifying.

"Now we are going to visualize first ourselves and then other individuals within the healing circle, picturing them for a few moments existing there in complete health, feeling very good and smiling. First of all, picture yourself inside the circle, completely whole and healed, happy and healthy." The leader instructs the group to say: "I place myself, (name), in the circle for healing." Each person in the circle repeats these words until everyone is in the circle.

The leader then instructs the participants as follows: "As you continue breathing, visualize others who require health and healing and say for each one: 'I place (name) in the circle for healing.'" This process does not have to go around the circle, and everyone can say this and name names at random.

"As you continue your mana breathing, keep filling the circle with mana. Then place the whole planet inside the circle, with all of its people, plants, and animals, existing in perfect harmony together, all happy and healthy. See the planet shining there in space, tranquil and at peace. Hold this vision for a while."

In closing, the leader asks everyone to raise their hands up together and repeat: "Let the mana created here be strong. Let it flow to the High Selves for the purpose of health and healing. Let the rain of blessings fall. So be it. It is done." (Use the rattle or drum in closing.)

Fire Ritual

The Fire Ritual is related to the act of creation. You are using the same power as does the goddess Pele, who transforms the earth with fire in order to create new land. In order to bring something into your life, transformation has to take place.

It is preferable to do this ritual at night, out-of-doors, with a group of like-minded people. A fire pit or brazier can be used. Take special safety precautions for yourself and the environment when working with fire out-of-doors.

Before starting the ritual, hand out small slips of paper and pencils to everyone in the group. In a contemplative state, have them write on a slip of paper the thing they want to come into their lives. Remind them of the Huna principle that one never interferes with another person's destiny and that all prayers are subject to self-sabotage if the proper clearing at the Basic Self level hasn't been done. The prayer-request is kept very simple, a few words at most. The participants do not discuss their prayer requests now or later.

When the fire is going well, form a circle around it (each person holds her own slip of paper). Use a conch, drum, rattle, or chant to begin the ritual.

The leader says, "We are gathered tonight to utilize the fires of creation to bring something new into our lives. For this, we ask that the High Selves of everyone be here to assist us, and we ask that the Basic Selves of everyone here please cooperate with us. We also ask the blessing of the goddess Pele, whose realm is fire and creation." (Use the drum or rattle again here.)

"Everyone in the circle, take four sets of four slow, deep mana breaths on your own, and visualize your prayer-request being granted. Picture what it would look like if it had already happened, and what your life would look like." Then, while beating the drum or rattling slowly, the leader instructs each person to approach the fire, one at a time, and stand before it, saying, "I, (name), give my request to the fire." The slip of paper is thrown into the fire. "So be it. It is done." After everyone in the group has thrown their papers into the fire, the leaders says: "Dearest High Selves, and dearest Pele, please take these requests into the fire and transform them into reality, for the highest good of all. We give you our sincere thanks. So be it. It is done."

Do a chant or song at this point, accompanied by the drum or rattle and end the ritual. It is not necessary to repeat this ritual. This is a powerful ritual that, when done with clarity and consciousness, is extremely effective.

Salt Ritual

To ritually cleanse your house of negative vibrations, charge salt with mana. Use any form of salt, though sea salt is preferable. First, strip the salt of its vibrations. To do this, go into the Silence with the salt in a bowl in front of you. Have a paper cup with water in it nearby. Ask both the High Self and the Basic Self to assist you.

Pass your hand over the salt in a sweeping motion, repeating, "This salt is being stripped of all vibrations." Fling the vibrations into the cup of water where they will be collected. Then, still in the Silence, take a series of four slow, deep mana breaths until you feel you have gathered a strong charge of mana to send to the High Self. It is preferable to charge the salt with both male and female energies, so it is best for both males and females to do the ritual together. Hold your hands over the salt, palms down and ask the High Self to direct the mana into the salt. Ask that the mana charging the salt be the purest, highest form of mana from the High Self.

Afterwards, throw the water with the discarded vibrations down the drain (not on plants). Discard the paper cup.

Wait until evening. Take the charged salt and sprinkle it lightly over your carpets and your furniture, though not on your television or electrical appliances. Don't put the salt in another's room without permission. Don't put it on houseplants or in pets' areas. While you are sprinkling the salt, say, "I purify this house for the highest good of all." Make sure you sprinkle it all throughout the house.

Do the ritual once a year or more often if there is negativity in the home or if negative people visit you. Cleanse the house after any incidents of disharmony such as arguments. You can purify your car with salt, but don't put salt on the dashboard or the ignition.

When charging salt, you can charge more than you need and save it for future occasions. If you are feeling unwell, put a bit of the charged salt in water and drink it, or add a small bit of it to your bath water.

ROSE LIGHT MEDITATION

Emotions emit vibrations that are expressed as color. Some very sensitive people can see the colors that surround a person. If you are having a problem with another person, the Rose Light Meditation taught by Josephine and Jack Gray is very effective. The rose color used in this meditation is a soft rose pink that represents impersonal divine love. When you do this meditation, you do not have to have the person's permission—this is not personal love but love from the High Self.

Go into the Silence and sit in a meditative position, preferably with a candle burning nearby. Take several sets of four slow, deep mana breaths. Ask your Basic Self and High Self to participate in the meditation. Picture a person you love in front of you. Visualize a beautiful soft pink rose light. When you have conjured the rose light, direct it to that person you love and see it surrounding them in a haze of beauty. Then, replace the person you love with the person with whom you have a problem. Hold the light around that person and see it permeating their very being until it fills the whole room and surrounds you, too.

At the point when you replace the person you love with the problem person, you may have difficulty sustaining the rose pink light (some people report that the light starts turning brown). It may help to have an object—a gemstone such as pink quartz or pink tourmaline or a piece of rose pink cloth—nearby as a visual aid. When other colors creep into the rose pink light, banish them and suffuse your image with shimmering rose pink light directly from the High Self. Maintain the rose pink light around both of you for several minutes. Then picture yourself shaking hands with the person or the two of you embracing. Smile at them and see them smiling back at you. Repeat this meditation several times if necessary. You should notice an immediate change in your relationship with the person.

SECRET SCRAPBOOK

Decide what you want to come into your life. Then buy a scrapbook or notebook. Cut out color pictures, letters, and numbers from magazines of things that symbolize what you wish to manifest, and paste them in the scrapbook. Don't see these pictures as specific, but rather as symbolic for what you want to manifest. For example, if you want a house, cut out a picture of a house that is close to the style and setting that you would like. Cut out letters to form a caption that says something like: "A LOVELY WELL-MADE AFFORDABLE HOUSE IN A RURAL AREA." You can include several things that you desire in your scrapbook at once. Put the scrapbook away in a place where it won't be disturbed, and don't mention it to anyone. After a moderate amount of time, such as six months, check the scrapbook to see what has manifested. Put new pictures in it then if you wish.

SOUL MATES

You may think you know what you want in a partner, but the High Self knows best. Instead of praying for someone specific to come along, make a prayer to the High Self for the right partner to appear at the right time. That way the High Self can arrange things for you. If you have difficulty in keeping relationships, look for the cause. Perhaps your Basic Self feels undeserving or is punishing you. Perhaps you are holding some destructive basic assumption about relationships or are repeating a dysfunctional pattern learned in your family. Look carefully at your past relationships to discern patterns in them and to understand the difficulties that arose. What blocks prevented you from having a good relationship? Once you have done the work to remove those blocks at the Basic Self level, ask the High Self to send you a compatible soul mate.

STONES AND ROCKS

In ancient Hawaii, stones and rocks were believed to have consciousness and to interact with the living. A Hawaiian saying went: *He ola ka pohaku*—There is life in the stone.[21] Rocks and formations could hold mana as well as spirits. Certain stones were sacred in themselves; others were special because of their association with a god, goddess, or person.

To work with stones, you must sensitize yourself to their energies. Practice communicating with stones at their level of consciousness, which is quite different from human or animal consciousness. Tune in to the slow, dense aliveness that is stone. Approach the stone with consideration and respect. First of all, never remove a stone from its native site without asking its permission. Should you wish to do so, hold your hand over the stone and ask silently if the stone wants to accompany you. If you are sensitive enough, you will get a definite answer. Then, when transporting it and placing it in its new home, treat the stone with loving care. Place it on your home altar and ask it to assist you in your spiritual work. When you gather mana, offer it some.

Over time, you will get a feeling for the interaction between you and the stone, and for the stone itself. If the interaction is working well for both of you, continue your interaction. Otherwise, return it to its original site or place it respectfully in your garden.

STRESS REDUCTION

From a Huna point of view, stress occurs for two basic reasons: one is an imbalance in the Selves in which the Basic Self's needs are not being met; the other derives from harmful assumptions at the Basic Self level that cause anxiety. In our fast-paced modern society, the Middle Selves tend to rule. The daily schedule includes prodigious amounts of work, numerous projects and activities, and the latest technology, all of which the Middle Self loves. The Middle Self constantly seeks mental diversion while the Basic Self seeks emotional equilibrium and physical diversion. Being with family and friends, listening to and making music, dancing, singing, art, participating in sports, hiking, gardening, and being out in nature are the kinds of activities the Basic Self enjoys. Sitting at a computer for hours and staring at a screen is usually not something that enhances the Basic Self. In fact, studies have shown that spending long hours on the Internet and watching lots of television do not promote mental health. They certainly do nothing for physical health. In a society increasingly dedicated to Middle Self activities, the Basic Self's needs are often slighted.

Why has this occurred? One reason is the number of choices available to the Middle Self today. In the past, simple pleasures like books and games provided mental diversions for the Middle Self. Today, there are multitudes of magazines, classes of every description, Internet chat rooms, and e-mail. The pressures to participate in all of these activities are strong and it is human nature to want to stay within the mainstream of society. There is, of course, nothing inherently bad about any of these things. Remember that Huna is a science of balance. Look at your daily schedule and determine which of the things you do serves the Middle Self and which the Basic Self. (Television and the Internet are mixed: they provide both entertainment and mental stimulation, but in a passive way that tends to drain mana.) Make a list of your daily activities, setting them down in two columns: Give Mana and Take Mana. The ones in the "Give" column are those that leave you feeling energized and the ones in the "Take" column leave you with low energy or feeling depleted of mana. Feeling physically tired after a hike or jog or a day's work is not the same as being depleted. Sensitize yourself to know the difference and to sense when something is draining your mana. After looking over this list, you may want to spend several hours a week less in front of television and go for a bicycle ride instead. Do things that build your mana on a daily basis and minimize the activities that drain it.

Make a list of activities your Basic Self would enjoy but that have been relegated to the back burner of your schedule. Then do an experiment for a month and substitute some of these activities for the ones you currently do. In general, rearrange your schedule to include more free time when you have nothing planned and no agenda. Let go of the feeling that you are "wasting time," since time given to the Basic Self to build mana is never wasted. The Puritan Ethic that says constant work is good can be a strong one. Revise it to a Huna Ethic in which play and rest for the Basic Self are essential to nourish a complete human being.

The other causes of stress are more complex and relate to your basic assumptions about yourself. For example, you may be a perfectionist and want your children, house, yard, and car to be in states of perfection at all times. This basic belief can cause a tremendous amount of stress as you work to achieve an impossible goal. In this case, dialoguing with the Basic Self to ease the demands of perfection helps. Remember that creativity flourishes when the drive for perfection ceases. Another source of stress is a need at the Basic Self level to meet others' demands. If you have difficulty saying no to demands on your time and find yourself involved in activities that deplete you, you are not nourishing your Basic Self. Life is best when it balances helping yourself and others. Responsibility can also be a source of stress for the Basic Self, especially when the responsible one feels inadequate and fears failure. Identifying basic fears underlying stress is the first step to alleviating it.

Other people can produce stress when they drain your mana. Make a list of the people in your life, putting them into "Give Mana" and "Take Mana" columns. The "Give Mana" ones are those who leave you feeling energized and cheerful after you've spent time with them. The "Take Mana" people literally take your mana away from you and leave you feeling tired and depressed. When you have this list done, evaluate the amount of time you currently allocate to both sides. It may be necessary in your life to spend some time with people who tend to drain your energy (such as unfavorite relatives, customers, or fellow employees), but you can learn to minimize the drainage by fortifying yourself with extra mana before being around them. Take several sets of slow, deep mana breaths for this purpose.

Your general goal in stress reduction is to alleviate daily tension that is generated by habitual activities, by your basic assumptions, and by others. There are always challenges in life. If you have peaceful and enjoyable aspects built into your life, however, you will have a greater store of mana to draw on when the challenges arise.

WEIGHT CHANGES

The body is the most vivid example of the ways in which you create your own reality. As a manifestation of the Basic Self, your body reflects your basic assumptions as well as your emotions. Issues of body weight can be tricky because they involve an activity—eating—that people do every day and one that is fraught with cultural attitudes as well as familial and personal habits. It is important to remember that every individual is different and has a unique set of beliefs that operate to determine behavior. Therefore, it is up to the individual to delve into his or her own psychological makeup in matters of weight.

As with any other situation, approach it from your knowledge of the Three Selves. First of all, determine whether or not it is really necessary for you to make changes in your body weight. This is important because, in a society that reveres impossibly thin supermodels, many distortions can occur. What often develops is a very oppressive "should" attitude toward weight that burdens the Basic Self with guilt, while there is no real agreement among the Selves on the subject. In fact, lack of harmony among the Selves is almost the norm in this issue. The Basic Self may feel guilty about not looking like a model, while the Middle Self may not see the value in making changes. On the other hand, the Middle and High Selves may recognize the benefit to your health in changing your weight, but at the same time, your Basic Self may have no interest whatsoever in acquiring new eating habits.

First assess the situation realistically, then bring your Selves into alignment. Using the reason of the Middle Self, discover whether or not you really need to change your body weight. It would be wise to consult a physician to discuss the needs of your body and to learn what your optimum weight really is. Visiting a physician or health professional also sends the message to your Basic Self that this is a serious issue worthy of assistance. Make sure when you get an assessment that such factors as body type, activity level, age, and physical condition are taken into account.

Then, if there truly is a need for change, look honestly at why your High, Middle, and Basic Selves are not working together to create an optimum body weight. This can be extremely complex. There are thousands of reasons why people eat food in ways that don't serve them. A person who feels like a victim may overeat to compensate for defeats. A person who feels unloved may "love" the Basic Self with food. Or, the opposite may occur. In one example, a woman who had been orphaned as a child was chronically underweight as an adult. She realized through therapy that she had acquired the habit of not eating enough from early childhood so that people would feel sorry for her and give her love and sympathy. When she began loving herself more, she began to realize a normal weight. Some people are very sensitive to those around them and "buffer" themselves with weight as a shield against the energy fields of others. These are just a few of the ways in which people are dysfunctional with food. Everyone, of course, has to contend with attitudes that are not constructive, often which were instilled by their families from an early age—attitudes about the selection, preparation, and eating of food. These are powerful patterns because they tie in with survival strategies at the Basic Self level.

Look carefully at your own patterns and those of your family. Consider your moment-to-moment feelings about food. What feelings cause you to make good choices and poor choices about food? Some people lose weight when they are stressed;

others gain. What is your pattern? Food intake, as well as the quality of food you eat, generally reflects your mental state. If you are overworked and tired a lot, you may overeat to gain energy, or you may avoid food. What is your mind/body mode of operating?

Overeating or eating inappropriate foods may indicate that the Middle Self is dominating the Basic Self. Here's how it works: the Middle Self's burdensome mental agendas give the Basic Self little time to rest and do things it enjoys. The Basic Self feels its needs are being suppressed, and the result is anxiety, stress, sleeplessness, and anger. To compensate, the Basic Self co-opts the basic activity of eating—the one activity that no one can avoid doing if they want to stay alive—by eating too much and too many "self-indulgent" foods. The "self" that is indulging is the Basic Self, and in this way, the Basic Self grabs a little enjoyment each mealtime. When the situation is understood, and when the Middle Self eases up and provides the Basic Self more leisure time in everyday life, the need to overeat and eat sweet/fatty/salty foods lessens. Giving more time to the Basic Self's overall needs is the key.

Bingeing is another way the Basic Self reacts to suppression by the Middle Self. If you have a basic assumption that you should look like a supermodel, your Basic Self is thrown completely out of balance. The basic assumption that you should be very thin conflicts with the desire to eat, and the Basic Self ends up at war with itself. Possibly, this can lead to anorexia or bulimia, which requires medical attention. The healing begins when the Basic Self and the Middle Self—with the help of the High Self—build a loving relationship based on caring rather than on "shoulds" and criticism. Blessing and loving the body at all times ultimately results in a far better physical being than criticism ever could produce.

Writing in a journal is a good way to discover your food patterns. Write down your feelings about food. Perhaps you will discern an area of disharmony in your makeup that you need to work on. Dialogue with your Selves to truly understand it. Then, work in the Silence or, if the problem is deep-seated, with a psychologist or hypnotherapist. Monitor yourself on a daily basis to see how you operate. Do you encounter a problem at work and then head for the candy machine? (In this case, stress has lowered your mana and caused the Basic Self to seek an instant energy source.) Do sensations of hunger occur when some other need is not being met? What kind of "nourishment" are you truly lacking? Is the hunger on a soul level? Does hunger itself give you a feeling of anxiety? Be very conscious of your thoughts and your behavior toward food.

Once you feel you understand your Basic Self's approach to food and your patterns, begin bringing the Selves into balance. The most important work you can do is on the "Self" level. Remember that it is the Middle Self's role to direct, but that direction without cooperation from the Basic Self is useless. The High Self provides the guidance.

The magic happens when you are conscious (and therefore can rid yourself) of harmful eating patterns at the Basic Self level, and both your Middle Self and Basic Self can agree to create a different way of living in your body. Ask for your

High Self's guidance, along with your spiritual guides, guardians, and angels. Dialogue with the Basic Self about its needs and desires. Ask for its sincere cooperation. When the Basic Self is cooperating in a desire to lose weight, there is no feeling of deprivation, only doing what all Three Selves desire.

If the Basic Self is uncertain or reluctant, do not be discouraged. Give it time. The Basic Self doesn't like change and usually resists it. Be very gentle and explain that a new way of being in your body is necessary for health and happiness. Be very honest and sincere with your Basic Self. Do not threaten or "beat yourself up"—this is not the way to achieve cooperation. Shower yourself with love and caring. Reinforce your guidance with affirmations and positive images of yourself.

When you feel that the Three Selves are in harmony about your goal, go into the Silence and ask your High Self and your guides, guardians, and angels to assist you in achieving a new physical state, happily and healthily. Ask that your body be in balance at all times. Also ask that people on the earth plane be sent to you to help you along your path. This can include physicians, hypnotherapists, health professionals, friends, coworkers, and family members. Ask, in fact, the whole universe to assist you in reaching your goal.

Problems can arise if your Basic Self has self-destructive complexes around food or drink that stem from fear. If fear is causing you to overeat, undereat, or to drink too much alcohol or coffee, you must deal with these fears on the Basic Self level. Do the following exercise: Keep a journal handy and when you head for the refrigerator at an inappropriate time, ask yourself,

"What is my fear?" Write down your fear. Take four slow, deep breaths. Then ask yourself: "What other thing can I do (besides eat or drink) to take away my fear?" Write this down also. If you have a desire to eat when you are feeling anxious, determine where your anxiety is coming from. Understand how this "dynamic" of anxiety = hunger is triggered within you. Experience the hunger or thirst as your Basic Self's need for comfort, love, and relief from fear. Gently tell your Basic Self that food or drink is not what you need right now. Speak softly to your Basic Self about the fear it is experiencing. Reassure it that all is well. Comfort it as you would a child.

When working with the Basic Self's hungers and cravings, you are dealing with a lifetime of conditioning at the Basic Self level. Give yourself time to re-orient your Basic Self to a new set of assumptions. Be very consistent over time in working with the Basic Self.

One note about diets—any new regime that you try, whether it is a prescribed diet or a diet plan you create yourself, changes the energy and makes an impression on the Basic Self. The Basic Self loves games, and a diet is often seen as a new game to play, thus the Basic Self cooperates with it at first. For this reason, diets may be successful initially and result in weight loss. After a while, however, the Basic Self tires of the game and reverts back to its old patterns. Nothing fundamental has shifted. When the Basic Self is truly convinced of the need for essential change, and fundamental fears are addressed, new patterns can be established for good.

Once your Basic Self has agreed to cooperate in creating a

new way of being in your body, do a ritual and visualization. A ritual for balance might go like this: Go into the Silence and ask your High Self to be present, along with your guides, guardians, and angels. Ask your Basic Self to be a part of the dialogue. "My dearest Basic Self, you are wonderful. You create and maintain our body with great skill and intelligence. I love you, and I really appreciate you. I know you want to live in happiness on this earth in complete balance. Therefore, let the High Self nourish us with wisdom and mana. Let us state our intention to nourish the body with good food, deep breathing, needed rest, and movement. Let us work together from now on in complete cooperation to create a happy, healthy body. Let us forever create balance and love in this life. So be it. It is done."

Visualize yourself in a state of optimum weight and health. See yourself as a shining, beautiful being.

Once you are in your new physical state, do a ritual in which you offer blessings and thanks to all of those—and especially to your Basic Self—who have brought it about. Visualize yourself smiling and happy, secure in your present way of being. See this process as an ongoing one in which you maintain optimum existence for all of your Selves. Above all, love yourself through this process.

Resources

HOW TO LEARN MORE ABOUT HUNA

Teachers in the Hawaiian tradition have been few, but their numbers are growing. If you desire to work with a teacher, look for someone who has a thorough understanding of Huna. In order to maintain a level of expertise and integrity, Huna Research Inc., the organization founded by Max Freedom Long, certifies Huna teachers and practitioners around the country and the world. Serge King's organization, Aloha International, trains teachers and therapists in his tradition, and these offer an active program of classes on a worldwide basis. Both organizations make available a large number of books and tapes for those who wish to learn that way. Among teachers of Huna, there is some variation, as individuals draw on their own traditions and the knowledge their teachers taught them. The organizations mentioned here are those known by the author to have a high degree of integrity, to have authentic Huna knowledge to impart, and to be accessible. Whether you journey to a seminar, listen to a tape while driving, or build a Huna library, there is a wealth of information for you to choose from. All of these sources are highly recommended.

Huna Research Inc. is a not-for-profit organization created by Max Freedom Long in 1945 for the purpose of disseminating information on Huna and providing a forum for those who practice it to share the results of their experience. Long encouraged those who read his first book on Huna, *Recovering the Ancient Magic,* to experiment with the concepts, and to add to the knowledge of Huna. (For an interesting narrative on the history of the development of Huna, read *The Story of the Huna Work* by E. Otha Wingo.) As Long continued to write books, he also issued a newsletter, called *Huna Vistas.* Before his death in 1971, Long asked E. Otha Wingo, a college professor living and teaching in Missouri, to continue the Huna work. Beginning on a shoestring, Wingo took on the huge task of reprinting and distributing Long's books, creating a correspondence course, and issuing newsletters, and beginning in 1975, holding annual Huna seminars. An accomplished speaker, Wingo has addressed audiences nationally and internationally about Huna for many years.

Today, Huna Research has a worldwide membership and represents an unbroken line that carries on the work that Max Freedom Long began. The organization has an active program of teacher training and certifies teachers who have demonstrated a knowledge of Huna, good character, and teaching ability. You can request a list of Certified Huna Teachers in your area. Huna training is accomplished through the correspondence course, *Letters on Huna: A Course in the Fundamentals of Huna Psychology,* by direct instruction at seminars on the mainland and in Hawaii, and through the extensive tapes and publications by a variety of authors that Huna Research makes available. *The Huna Work International,* a journal of articles and news about Huna, is published quarterly. Write for a free copy of the booklet, *Huna Psychology,* and a free copy of the Huna Ha Rite Flowchart. E. Otha Wingo continues to direct the organization while his son, Vinson Wingo, administers it. Huna Research Inc., 1760 Anna St., Cape Girardeau, Missouri 63701-4504; tel. (573) 334-3478; e-mail: Huna@mail.com; website: www.huna-research.com.

Aloha International is the worldwide network of teachers and members founded by Serge Kahili King to bring Hawaiian knowledge to a wide audience. King was trained in the Hawaiian tradition and has, over the years, established himself as an important interpreter and teacher of Hawaiian shamanic wisdom. He is the author of a number of excellent books, including *Kahuna Healing, Mastering Your Hidden Self: A Guide to the Huna Way,* and *Urban Shaman.* His organization, based in Kilauea, Hawaii, on the island of Kauai, offers workshops and training there and around the world, as well as many publications, video and audiotapes, and a variety of related products. You can request a list of Huna teachers and therapists, as well as workshops. An active website presents information about all of these. King is astute in explaining Huna concepts and can distill Hawaiian wisdom and present it in a very accessible way. He and his staff and teachers have created an essential body of Huna knowledge that includes such subjects as relationships, success, healing, and energy. Request a Huna By Mail catalog. Aloha International, P.O. Box 665, Kilauea, Kauai, Hawaii 96754; tel./fax: (808) 828-0302; e-mail: huna@aloha.net; websites: http://www.huna.org (Hawaiian Huna Village) and http://www.huna.net (Huna By Mail).

The Heart of Huna was founded by Laura Kealoha Yardley for the purpose of teaching and allowing others to experience Huna. Yardley was born and raised in Hawaii and derives her intuitive knowledge of Huna from her Hawaiian grandmother Puna. She combines the spiritual source of her ancestors with an extensive study of all forms of Huna to teach a heart-based Huna. In true Hawaiian tradition, she teaches the interconnectedness of all things, the meaning of ohana, the ha breath, empowerment, prayer, and chanting. She has a special connection to the goddess Uli, who manifests as the feminine creative force. Yardley's book *The Heart of Huna,* presents her own story, along with basic information on the teachings of Max Freedom Long and David Kaonohiokala Bray. Her organization offers seminars and workshops in Hawaii, California, Canada, and the South Pacific. The Heart of Huna, P.O. Box 280, Ashland, Oregon 97520; tel. (541) 201-0712; e-mail: kealoha@ mindspring.com.

The Huna World Alliance Inc., based in Canada, holds seminars and workshops and sponsors study groups. The organization is "dedicated to the purpose of researching and making the miracles and magic of the ancient Polynesian belief system work with full effectiveness in our Western culture." This not-for-profit organization has memberships and publishes *Showers of Mana,* a quarterly newsletter containing articles and information. It is headed by Stevan Varro, a long-time Huna practitioner and teacher. Huna World Alliance Headquarters, 2838-26A Street SW, Calgary, Alberta, Canada T3E 2C9; tel. (403) 246-1080; e-mail: Huna@cadvision.com.

Vector Counseling Institute, 1065-388 Lomita Blvd., Harbor City, California; 90710; tel. (310) 539-3922; and Vector Counseling Institute, P.O. Box 29779, Los Angeles, California 90029. Vector counseling is an effective means of clearing out harmful patterns and assumptions from the Basic Self and provides a good complement to Huna work. The method is summarized in the book *Huna Magic* by John Bainbridge and is treated at length in the book *Fill Your Bowl with Cherries* by Ben Keller. Both books are available from Huna Research Inc.

Kellie Koucky, Spirit Chants, 2208 Bishop Ave., Fremont, California 94536; tel. (510) 791-8305; e-mail: kkoucky@ hotmail.com. Kellie Koucky is a Certified Huna Teacher and Reiki Master who offers spirit chant creation and counseling in person and by telephone.

TOOLS FOR PRACTITIONERS

There are several sources for products designed to go along with Huna practices. Some of these are helpful in communicating with the Basic Self and the High Self, while others are useful energetically. Serge King's organization (Aloha International) makes available the Shaman Stones for receiving advice and guidance, the Amazing Managizer, Shaman Power Patterns, a Power Coin, and Power Sticks.

Laura Kealoha Yardley (The Heart of Huna) creates beautiful Spirals of Aloha—spiral bracelets from natural stones and other natural materials made while she is in meditation. Both men and women can use them to enhance their mana.

An excellent set of cards entitled Pacific Voyager Cards— Journey to Kanaka Makua: Rediscovering the Light of Island Wisdom—has been created by Greg Scott to facilitate higher guidance. They help in "visioning, purposing, and transformation." Greg Scott, P.O. Box 1722, Keaau, Hawaii 96749; tel. (808) 968-7164; e-mail: gscott@interpac.net.

A number of Huna practitioners use Tarot cards in their Huna work, and Max Freedom Long wrote of links between Huna and Tarot. He called Tarot a "magical" truth and a valuable tool and interpreted the cards for Huna students in his book on the subject.

Whatever tools you choose, whether pendulum, cards, stones, or something you devise yourself, remember that these are a fun and dramatic means of communicating with your Selves. Experiment with tools and see what works for you.

SOURCES FOR THIS BOOK

The sources for this book are numerous. One of the most profound sources was the work of David Kaonohiokala "Daddy" Bray, mentioned elsewhere in this text. Daddy Bray was a very unusual kahuna in his desire and willingness to pass on his knowledge to non-Hawaiians. To keep Hawaiian wisdom from being lost, he led seminars in California and Hawaii and trained teachers who in turn trained other teachers. I studied with several of Daddy Bray's students and was privileged to have attended two seminars in Hawaii in which his son, David M. Bray, was a teacher. In addition, I have received knowledge in person from other teachers in the Hawaiian tradition such as Morrnah Simeona, Abraham Kawai'i, Laura Kealoha Yardley, Pali Jae Lee, and Koko Willis. The annual seminars held by Huna Research Inc. under the direction of E. Otha Wingo have introduced me to a wide variety of practitioners and teachings over the years.

My most extensive training was with Josephine and Jack Gray, Huna teachers in San Francisco whose Institute of Balance was the focal point for Huna in the Bay Area for many years. For several years during the 1980s, I attended their classes as well as their regular Inner Circle gatherings for advanced students. Many of the techniques and ideas presented in this book are derived from their teachings, and these were derived in part from one of their teachers, Clark Wilkerson. These teachings are very close to the ones described in two books by Allan P. Lewis, *Living in Harmony Through Kahuna Wisdom* and *Clearing Your Lifepath Through Kahuna Wisdom*. Both books are highly recommended for further study.

I followed one rule in writing this book: all of the techniques are ones I have personally used and experienced. I have known

223

others who have used them successfully as well. Since Huna was made known to people around the world, generations of students have tested its methods and found benefit in them. The proof is in the doing and in the results.

This book is intended as an introduction and guide to Huna that gives the novice both a basis for understanding and a handy reference tool. For those of you who find Huna speaks to you and who choose to walk its path, I commend you and encourage you. Huna requires personal responsibility and a willingness to ascend to a higher way of thinking and living. I wish you abundant mana and warm aloha.

REFERENCES

(1) Herb Kawainui Kane. *Ancient Hawai'i*, 1997, p. 10–17.

(2) Martha Warren Beckwith (trans. and ed.). *The Kumulipo: A Hawaiian Creation Chant*, 1951, p. 51.

(3) Martha Beckwith. *Hawaiian Mythology*, 1970, p. 12–13.

(4) David K. "Daddy" Bray. *Lessons for a Kahuna*, 1985, p. 1.

(5) Mary Kawena Pukui and Alfons L. Korn. *The Echo of Our Song*, 1973, p. 42–47.

(6) Charles W. Kenn (Arii-Peu Tama-iti). *Fire-Walking from the Inside*, 1949, p. 43.

(7) Max Freedom Long. *The Secret Science Behind Miracles*, 1982, p. 1.

(8) Ibid., p. 366.

(9) Ibid., p. 14.

(10) Max Freedom Long. *Mana or Vital Force*, 1981, p. 30.

(11) John Bainbridge. *Huna Magic*, 1988, p. 67–88

(12) Mary Kawena Pukui and Samuel H. Elbert. *Hawaiian Dictionary*, p. 341.

(13) Mary Kawena Pukui, E.W. Haertig, and Catherine A. Lee. *Nana I Ke Kumu (Look to the Source)*, Vol. I, 1983, p. 70.

(14) Mary Kawena Pukui, E.W. Haertig, and Catherine A. Lee. *Nana I Ke Kumu (Look to the Source)*, Vol. II, 1979, p. 11–12.

(15) E. Victoria Shook. *Ho'oponopono*, 1985, p. 11–12.

(16) Pukui, Haertig & Lee. Vol. I, p. 78.

(17) Allan P. Lewis. *Clearing Your Lifepath Through Kahuna Wisdom*, 1983, p. 135.

(18) David Kaonohiokala Bray and Douglas Low. *The Kahuna Religion of Hawaii*, 1990, p. 47.

(19) Betty Bethards. *The Dream Book: Symbols for Self-Understanding*, 1986.

(20) Allen Lawrence and Lisa Lawrence. *Huna: Ancient Miracle Healing Practices and the Future of Medicine*, 1994.

(21) Van James. *Ancient Sites of Hawai'i*, 1998, p. 31.

APPENDIX

The Language of Huna

It is not necessary to use Hawaiian words when practicing Huna, but they are so intertwined with Huna's source and concepts that a few notes of clarification may be in order.

Max Freedom Long spent years analyzing the meanings of Hawaiian words, breaking them into their component parts to look for deeper meanings. For this task, he used a Hawaiian dictionary compiled by Lorrin Andrews (1795–1868), a respected missionary and teacher. Based on a smaller dictionary that Andrews had compiled in 1838, this edition, called *A Dictionary of the Hawaiian Language,* was published in 1865. A major revision of the work in 1922, long after Andrews' death, changed many definitions and omitted words considered unsuitable for print. Arriving in Hawaii in 1917, Long had access to the older 1865 version.

It is rewarding for the student of Huna to take a closer look at the vocabulary of Huna. Good books for this are Andrews' dictionary, the contemporary *Hawaiian Dictionary* by Mary Kawena Pukui and Samuel H. Elbert, and an excellent set of references: *Nana I Ke Kumu (Look to the Source)* in two volumes (Volume I is especially useful in this regard). Serge King has very perceptive comments on the concepts and meanings of Hawaiian words in his series of books.

According to the 1865 edition of the Andrews dictionary, the noun "huna" means "that which is concealed," and the verb means "to hide or conceal." The word also contains the meaning of "to protect and defend." "Mana" is defined as "supernatural power," and "an attribute of the gods," with the associations of power, strength, and authority.

"Ha" means to breathe but with the connotation of "breathing strongly," rather than normal breathing. It is also the word for the number four, and it is significant that four and its multiples were considered sacred numbers by the Hawaiians.

"Kala," a verb, is "to loosen, untie," and "to forgive." It involves a mutual letting go of a grievance in which both the wronged and the guilty take the necessary steps. Kala involves confession and restitution and is an important aspect of ho'oponopono, the resolving of family problems. Ho'oponopono, a verb, may require some practice in order to pronounce. It means "to rectify"—to set right.

In describing the Three Selves, Max Freedom Long used the word "Aumakua" to refer to the High Self, translating it as "the older, entirely trustworthy parental self." That it is a personal god to the Hawaiians is clear, but it is also defined as an ancestor spirit, or more precisely, a spirit being from one's lineage. The Aumakua, in its role of a guiding, protective spirit, can take the form of an animal or other element of nature and intercede for the living with the *Akua,* or impersonal gods. *Unihipili,* which Long used to describe the Basic Self, generally has the meaning of a recently deceased spirit, especially one residing in the bones, that was called upon to help the living. The word Long used for the Middle Self, the *Uhane,* was the spirit of a person that could live on after death, retaining aspects of the personality and revisiting persons and places. In other terminology and with a

228

rough parallel to Long's Three Selves, Serge King refers in his books to three "aspects of consciousness," calling them Kane (High), Lono (Middle), and Ku (Basic or Low) (See his *Urban Shaman,* 1990, pg. 36, for an explanation).

Long described the mana used by the Three Selves as having different frequencies: the Basic Self gathers *mana;* the Middle Self uses *mana-mana* for mental activity, which becomes *mana-loa* at the High Self level.

Long deciphered Hawaiian words by breaking them down to their component parts, and this analysis yielded for him an understanding of their esoteric meanings. These ancient Hawaiian words, however, are fraught with lore, multiple meanings, and many different cultural interpretations. Different teachers and writers use them in different ways. It is therefore simpler to render the concepts, with a few exceptions, with their English equivalents.

The rituals in this book end with the words, "So be it. It is done." This is a non-literal rendering of the ending of many Hawaiian prayers: *Amama. Ua noa.* The words literally mean: "The kapu is lifted. The prayer is free." In other words, the prayer has no restrictions that would block it from flying to its destination.

HAWAIIAN GLOSSARY

aka – essence, shadow

akua – impersonal god, spirit consciousness

ala – path or way

ali'i – ruler, royalty

aloha – love, greetings

aloha aina – love for the land

amama – ended (said of a prayer)

aumakua – personal god, ancestral spirit

awa – *(Piper methysticum),* also known as kava, a non-addictive drink used by the kahuna ceremonially and to induce an altered state

ha – breath, the numeral four

hale – house

hana – work

haole – foreigner

hau'oli – happy

heiau – temple of the Hawaiian islands

hoku – star

honua – earth

ho'oponopono – to make things right, family process for resolving problems

hui – group

hula – dance, sacred dance

huna – secret, to conceal

ike – spiritual knowledge, awareness, or power

ilima – Hawaiian shrub *(Sida)* with yellow/orange flowers *inoa* – name

ipu – gourd

kahiko – old, ancient

kahu – guardian, caretaker

kahuna – master, expert, shaman, priest

kahuna ana'ana – sorcerer

kahuna lapa'au – healer, medical practitioner

kahuna pule – prayer expert

kai – sea water

kala – untie, forgive, cleanse

kane – male

kapu – sacred, forbidden, taboo

kaula – prophet

kiawe – Algaroba tree *(Prosopis pallida)*

ki'i – image

kino – body, self

kino lau – the many forms that could be taken by a spirit being

koa – native hardwood of Hawaii *(Acacia koa),* brave

kokua – help

ku – to stand or rise upright; *Ku* – Hawaiian deity

kukui – candlenut *(Aleurites moluccana),* light

kumu – teacher, source

kupua – spirit being

kupuna – grandparent, ancestor

la – sun

lani – sky, heavenly

lapa'au – herbal healing

lehua – flower of the ohi'a tree *(Metrosideros macropus) lei* – garland

lomilomi – massage

lono – news; Lono – Hawaiian deity

lu'au – feast, taro tops

mahalo – thanks, gratitude

mahina – moon

maika'i – good, fine

maile – a fragrant vine (*Alyxia olivaeformis*)

makani – wind

makua – parent

mana – spiritual power, vital life force

manu – bird

mauna – mountain

mele – chant, song

menehune – an early race of people living in the Hawaiian islands

moana – ocean

moe uhane – dream

noa – freedom; freed of taboo

noho – seat, possession by a spirit or a god

ohana – family

oki – to cut

ola – life, health

olelo – language, word

olena (turmeric) *(Curcuma domestica)* – mixed with water, it was used ceremonially

pahu – drum

pau – finished

Po'e Aumakua – Great Company of High Selves

pohaku – stone

pono – right, order

pua – flower

pule – prayer

pu'uhonua – sanctuary

taro (kalo) (Colocasia esculenta) – the most important food
source plant of the Hawaiians, its root was used to make
poi

tapa (kapa) – barkcloth made from the paper mulberry tree

ti (ki) – *(Cordyline terminalis)* a plant of the lily family used for
protection and whose leaves are used in ritual

ua – rain

uhane – soul or spirit

unihipili – spirit of the deceased, often residing in bones

wa'a – canoe

wahine – female

wai – fresh water, liquid

BIBLIOGRAPHY

By Max Freedom Long:

Recovering the Ancient Magic. Cape Girardeau, MO: Huna Press, 1978.

The Secret Science Behind Miracles. Marina del Rey, CA: DeVorss & Co., 1948.

The Secret Science at Work. Marina del Rey, CA: DeVorss & Co., 1953

Growing into Light. Marina del Rey, CA: DeVorss & Co., 1955.

Self-Suggestion and the New Huna Theory of Mesmerism and Hypnosis. Marina Del Rey, CA: DeVorss & Co., 1958.

Psychometric Analysis. Marina del Rey, CA: DeVorss & Co., 1959.

The Huna Code in Religions. Marina del Rey, CA: DeVorss & Co., 1965.

Mana or Vital Force. Cape Girardeau, MO: Huna Research, 1981.

Tarot Card Symbology. Cape Girardeau, MO: Huna Press, 1983.

What Jesus Taught in Secret. Marina del Rey, CA: DeVorss & Co., 1983.

By and about David Kaonohiokala Bray:

The Kahuna Religion of Hawaii, by David K. Bray and Douglas Low. Garberville, CA: Borderland Sciences, 1960 & 1990.

Lessons for a Kahuna, by David K. Bray. Pasadena, CA, 1967 and Kailua-Kona, HI, 1985.

Berney, Charlotte, "David Kaonohiokala Bray: A Hawaiian Kahuna," in *Shamans of the 20th Century*, ed. by Ruth-Inge Heinze. New York: Irvington Publishers, 1991.

By Allan P. Lewis:

Clearing Your Lifepath Through Kahuna Wisdom. Las Vegas, NV: Homana Pub., 1983.

Living in Harmony Through Kahuna Wisdom. Las Vegas, NV: Homana Pub., 1984.

By Serge Kahili King:

Imagineering for Health. Wheaton, IL: Theosophical Pub. House, 1981.

Kahuna Healing. Wheaton, IL: Theosophical Pub. House, 1983.

Mastering Your Hidden Self: A Guide to the Huna Way. Wheaton, IL: Theosophical Pub. House, 1985.

Urban Shaman, New York: Simon & Schuster, 1990.

Miscellaneous authors:

Andrews, Lorrin. *A Dictionary of the Hawaiian Language.* Rutland, VT: Chas. Tuttle Co., 1980.

Bainbridge, John. *Huna Magic.* Los Angeles, CA: Barnhart Press, P.O. Box 27940, 1994.

Beckwith, Martha Warren (trans. and ed.). *The Kumulipo: A Hawaiian Creation Chant.* Honolulu: Univ. Press of Hawaii, 1951.

Beckwith, Martha. *Hawaiian Mythology.* Honolulu: Univ. Press of Hawaii, 1970.

Bethards, Betty. *The Dream Book: Symbols for Self-Understanding*. Novato, CA: Inner Light Foundation, 1986.

Charlot, John. *Chanting the Universe: Hawaiian Religious Culture*. Honolulu: Emphasis Intl., 1983.

Chun, Malcolm (trans.). *Hawaiian Medicine Book*. Honolulu: Bess Press, 1986.

Cunningham, Scott. *Hawaiian Religion & Magic*. St. Paul, MN: Llewellyn Publications, 1995.

Dudley, Michael Kioni. *Man, Gods, and Nature*. Honolulu: Ka Nane O Ka Malo Press, 1990.

Glover, William. *Huna—The Ancient Religion of Positive Thinking*. Cape Girardeau, MO: Huna Press, 1983.

Gutmanis, June. *Kahuna Laʻau Lapaʻau*. Honolulu: Island Heritage, 1985.

Gutmanis, June. *Na Pule Kahiko—Ancient Hawaiian Prayers*. Honolulu: Editions Ltd., 1983.

Gutmanis, June. *Pohaku—Hawaiian Stones*. Laie, Hawaii: Brigham Young University, n.d.

Heinze, Ruth-Inge. *Shamans of the 20th Century*. New York, NY: Irvington Publishers, 1991.

Hoffman, Enid. *Huna: A Beginner's Guide*. Rockport, MA: Para Research, 1981.

James, Van. *Ancient Sites of Hawaiʻi, Archaeological Places of Interest on the Big Island*. Honolulu: Mutual Publishing, 1995.

Kamakau, Samuel Manaiakalani. *Ka Poʻe Kahiko—The People of Old*. Honolulu: Bishop Museum Press, 1979.

Kane, Herb Kawainui. *Ancient Hawai'i*. Captain Cook, HI: The Kawainui Press, 1997.

Kane, Herb Kawainui. *Pele-Goddess of Hawai'i's Volcanoes*. Captain Cook, HI: The Kawainui Press, 1987.

Keller, Ben. *You Can Fill Your Bowl with Cherries*. Harbor City, CA: Vector Counseling Institute, 1999.

Kenn, Charles W. (Arii-Peu Tama-iti), *Fire-Walking from the Inside*. Cape Girardeau, MO: Huna Research, Inc., 1949.

Lawrence, Allen and Lisa Lawrence. *Huna: Ancient Miracle Healing Practices and the Future of Medicine*. New York: Hanover House, 1994.

Lee, Pali, and Koko Willis. *Tales from the Night Rainbow*. Honolulu: Willis Ohana, 1986.

Macdonald, Arlyn J. *Inneractive Huna: A Guide for Self-Discovery Using the Secret Teachings of the Ancient Hawaiians*. Montrose, CO: Inner Power & Light Co., 1998.

Malo, David. *Hawaiian Antiquities*. Honolulu: Bishop Museum Press, 1980.

McBride, L.R. *The Kahuna-Versatile Mystics of Old Hawaii*. Hilo, HI: The Petroglyph Press, n.d.

Melville, Leinani. *Children of the Rainbow*. Wheaton, IL: The Theosophical Pub. House, 1969.

Nau, Erika S. *Huna Self-Awareness*. York Beach, ME: Samuel Weiser, 1992.

Parsons, Claire D.F. *Healing Practices in the South Pacific*. Honolulu: University of Hawaii Press, 1995.

Pukui, Mary Kawena, E. W. Haertig and Catherine A. Lee. *Nana I Ke Kumu (Look to the Source)*, Vol. I & Vol. II. Honolulu: Queen Lili'uokalani Children's Center, 1972 and 1979.

Pukui, Mary and Alfons L. Korn (trans. and ed.) *The Echo of Our Song: Chants and Poems of the Hawaiians.* Honolulu: Univ. of Hawaii Press, 1979.

Pukui, Mary Kawena and Samuel H. Elbert. *Hawaiian Dictionary.* Honolulu: University of Hawaii Press, 1986.

Rodman, Julius. *The Kahuna Sorcerers of Hawaii, Past and Present.* Hicksville, NY: Exposition Press, 1979.

Shook, E. Victoria. *Ho'oponopono.* Honolulu: University of Hawaii Press, 1985.

Steiger Brad. *Kahuna Magic.* Rockport, MA: Para Research, 1971.

Vilenskaya, Larissa and Joan Steffy. *Firewalking: A New Look at an Old Enigma.* Falls Village, CN: The Bramble Co., 1991.

Wilkerson, Clark. *Hawaiian Magic.* Honolulu: Institute of Cosmic Wisdom, 1965.

Wingo, E. Otha. *The Story of the Huna Work.* Cape Girardeau, MO: Huna Research, 1981.

Yardley, Laura Kealoha. *The Heart of Huna.* Honolulu: Advanced Neuro Dynamics, Inc. 1982.

Zambucka, Kristin. *Ano Ano (The Seed).* Honolulu: Mana Pub. Co., 1978.

INDEX

239

BOOKS BY THE CROSSING PRESS

OTHER BOOKS IN THE SERIES

Fundamentals of Jewish Mysticm and Kabbalah

By Ron Feldman

This concise introductory book explains what Kabbalah is and how study of its text and practices enhance the life of the soul and the holiness of the body.

$12.95 • Paper • ISBN 1-58091-049-1

Fundamentals of Tibetan Buddhism

By Rebecca McClen Novick

This book explores the history, philosophy, and practice of Tibetan Buddhism. Novick's concise history of Buddhism, and her explanations of the Four Noble Truths, Wheel of Life, Karma, Five Paths, Six Perfections, and the different schools of thought within the Buddhist teachings help us understand Tibetan Buddhism as a way of experiencing the world, more than as a religion or philosophy.

$12.95 • Paper • ISBN 0-89594-953-9

OTHER BOOKS BY THE CROSSING PRESS

A Woman's I Ching

By Diane Stein

A feminist interpretation of the popular ancient text for diving the character of events. Stein's version reclaims the feminine, or yin, content of the ancient work and removes all oppressive language and imagery.

$16.95 • Paper • ISBN 0-89594-857-5

All Women Are Psychics

By Diane Stein

Women's intuition is no myth; women really are psychic. But your inborn psychic sense was probably suppressed when you were very young. This inspiring book will help you rediscover and reclaim your dormant psychic aptitude.

$16.95 • Paper • ISBN 0-89594-979-2

BOOKS BY THE CROSSING PRESS

Channeling for Everyone: A Safe Step-by-Step Guide to Developing Your Intuition and Psychic Awareness

By Tony Neate

This is a clear, concise guide to developing our subtler levels of consciousness. It provides us with safe, step-by-step exercises to prepare for and begin to practice channeling, allowing wider states of consciousness to become part of our everyday lives.

$12.95 • Paper • ISBN 0-89594-922-9

Clear Mind, Open Heart: Healing Yourself, Your Relationships and the Planet

By Eddie and Debbie Shapiro

The Shapiros offer an uplifting, inspiring, and deeply sensitive approach to healing through spiritual awareness. Includes practical exercises and techniques to help us all in making our own journey.

$16.95 • Paper • ISBN 0-89594-917-2

Ghosts, Spirits and Hauntings

By Patricia Telesco

Ghosts, specters, phantoms, shades, spooks, or wraiths-no matter what the name, Patricia Telesco will help you identify and cope with their presence. Whatever you encounter, Patricia would like you to relate to it sensitively and intelligently, using this book as a guide.

$10.95 • Paper • ISBN 0-89594-871-0

The Heart of the Circle: A Guide to Drumming

By Holly Blue Hawkins

Holly Blue Hawkins will walk you through the process of finding a drum, taking care of it, calling a circle, setting an intention, and drumming together. She will also show you how to incorporate drumming into your spiritual practice. She offers you an invitation to explore rhythm in a free and spontaneous manner.

$12.95 • Paper • ISBN 1-58091-025-4

BOOKS BY THE CROSSING PRESS

The Native American Sweat Lodge: History and Legends
By Joseph Bruchac

To deepen our understanding of the significance of sweat lodges within Native American cultures, Bruchac shares 25 relevant traditional tales from the Lakota, Blackfoot, Hopi, and others.—Booklist

$12.95 • Paper • ISBN 0-89594-636-X

Peace Within the Stillness:
Relaxation & Meditation for True Happiness
By Eddie and Debbie Shapiro

Meditation teachers Eddie and Debbie Shapiro teach a simple, ancient practice which will enable you to release even deeper levels of inner stress and tension. Once you truly relax, you will enter the quiet mind and experience the profound, joyful, and healing energy of meditation.

$14.95 • Paper • ISBN 0-89594-926-1

Physician of the Soul: *A Modern Kabbalist's Approach to Health and Healing*
By Rabbi Joseph H. Gelberman with Lesley Sussman

In a self-awareness program suitable for all faiths, internationally renowned Rabbi Joseph Gelberman reveals wisdom drawn from Jewish mysticism. Exercises in meditation, visualization, and prayer are discussed to promote harmony in mind, body, and soul.

$14.95 • Paper • ISBN 1-58091-061-0

Pocket Guide to Celtic Spirituality
By Sirona Knight

The Earth-centered philosophy and rituals of ancient Celtic spirituality have special relevance today as we strive to balance our relationship with the planet. This guide offers a comprehensive introduction to the rich religious tradition of the Celts.

$6.95 • Paper • ISBN 0-89594-907-5

BOOKS BY THE CROSSING PRESS

Pocket Guide to Meditation

By Alan Pritz

This book focuses on meditation as part of spiritual practice, as a universal tool to forge a deeper connection with spirit. In Alan Pritz's words, Meditation simply delivers one of the most purely profound experiences of life, joy.

$6.95 • Paper • ISBN 0-89594-886-9

Pocket Guide to Self Hypnosis

By Adam Burke, Ph. D.

Self-hypnosis and imagery are powerful tools that activate a very creative quality of mind. By following the methods provided, you can begin to make progress on your goals and feel more in control of your life and destiny.

$6.95 • Paper • ISBN 0-89594-824-9

Pocket Guide to Visualization

By Helen Graham

Visualization is imagining; producing mental images that come to mind as pictures we can see. These pictures can help you relax, assess and manage stress, improve self-awareness, alleviate disease and manage pain.

$6.95 • Paper • ISBN 0-89594-885-0

Shamanism as a Spiritual Practice for Daily Life

By Tom Cowan

This inspirational book blends elements of shamanism with inherited traditions and contemporary religious commitments. An inspiring spiritual call.—Booklist

$16.95 • Paper • ISBN 0-89594-838-9

To receive a current catalog from The Crossing Press
please call toll-free, 800-777-1048.
Visit our Web site: **www.crossingpress.com**